chew on this

31 BIBLICAL DEVOTIONS
INTO THE HEART OF CHRIST

DAVE AMBROSE

chew on this

31 BIBLICAL DEVOTIONS
INTO THE HEART OF CHRIST

CD INCLUDED

DAVE AMBROSE

 ZONDERVAN®

ZONDERVAN.com/
AUTHORTRACKER
follow your favorite authors

 invert

 youth
specialties

**youth
specialties**

Chew on This: 31 Biblical Devotions into the Heart of Christ
Copyright 2007 by Dave Ambrose

Youth Specialties products, 300 S. Pierce St., El Cajon, CA 92020 are published
by Zondervan, 5300 Patterson Ave. SE, Grand Rapids, MI 49530.

Library of Congress Cataloging-in-Publication Data

Ambrose, Dave.
  Chew on this! : 30 biblical devotions into the heart of Christ / Dave
Ambrose.
      p. cm.
  ISBN-10: 0-310-27922-4 (pbk.)
  ISBN-13: 978-0-310-27922-8 (pbk.)
  1. Christian teenagers—Religious life. 2. Devotional literature. I.
Title.
  BV4531.3.A43 2007
  242'.63—dc22

2007037120

Cover design by Toolbox Studios
Interior design by David Conn

Printed in the United States of America

07 08 09 10 11 12 • 18 17 16 15 14 13 12 11 10 9 8 7 6 5 4 3 2 1

This book is dedicated to...

...my wonderful wife, Melody, and my two boys, Josh and Ty. Thanks for always encouraging me to pursue my dreams! They've all come true by being a part of your lives.

Thanks to...

...Tic Long for believing in me enough to invite me to be a part of everything God continues to do through Youth Specialties. Thanks also to Patty McCaulay, Angie Adams, and Brent Bill for all of your help reviewing this book. May Jesus Christ be lifted up and honored as a result of our labor.

Contents

Read This First—
The Purpose of This Book
(and How to Use It)

Both of my boys have incredible imaginations.

My younger son Tyler likes to use his imagination when he's playing with his action figures. I love listening to the different voices he uses before he falls asleep at night. The best ones are when the rubber snakes are eating all of the village people who can't seem to escape no matter how fast they try to run away. In the morning, his bed is covered with all sorts of make-believe items that were a part of his imaginary epic battle the night before.

My older son Josh, on the other hand, uses his imagination when he dreams. I love listening to his stories when he wakes up. I never know if he actually had a dream or if he's making it up as he goes. Either way, it's very entertaining! Last week he told me about a dream where he was in a boxing ring fighting off pepperonis and cheeseburgers that were attacking him and trying to take him away to their castle. He managed to defeat them, but not before a giant clown came down and started licking his face.

Believe it or not, when it comes to our spiritual lives, our imaginations are very useful. That's not something you may be used to hearing, but our imaginations are very valuable tools in helping us become better followers of Jesus. When we use our imaginations, our world takes on a different dimension. Imagination allows us to dream about things that haven't been created yet, to envision ourselves and others in different places and circumstances, even to discover things about ourselves that will be pivotal in our journey toward God.

Guided Meditation

What's the first thing that comes to mind when you hear the word *meditation*? If you're like me, you get an image of some guy sitting cross-legged with his eyes closed, his arms spread out with his palms facing upward, humming to himself. While that may be an accurate picture for some religions, this isn't at all what guided meditations are about in Christianity.

First of all, in the Bible, the word *meditate*, as best we can tell, literally means "to chew upon" over and over again—kind of like the way a dog chews on a bone. On special occasions, I give my dog Raider a nice big soup bone. I love watching him as he gnaws it over and over again, mulling it over in his mouth until he scrapes every last possible piece of meat off it. This is the image the Bible gives us for what it means to meditate: To "chew upon" God's truth over and over again until we get every last ounce of nourishment from it. (Hence the title of this book!)

The Bible is meant to give us strength and to help us become more and more like Jesus himself. The Bible wasn't written to make us smarter. It wasn't written so that we could impress our friends with how many verses we've memorized or how much we know about God. The Word of God is meant to be consumed and digested. It's meant to help us grow and transform into the kind of people we were created to be from the very beginning—people who live like Jesus and conduct themselves based on the truth that he's here today, living in our souls. That's the goal, isn't it? To imitate him in every way? Only when we learn to live like that will we ever truly be fulfilled.

Now, the guided meditations in this book are different from Bible meditations: When you meditate on Scripture, you focus on and enter into the narrative of the biblical text; the subject matter of the guided mediations in this book are much broader—you'll imagine yourself in various scenes and circumstances, sensing and responding to the images you see in your mind's eye and the emotions they bring. Then after you've completed your Guided Mediation, you have the chance to write about what you experienced and connect it with Scripture.

The reason we're using Guided Meditations in this book is because I've found them to be exciting tools for engaging the imagination—they bring the Word of God to life in ways that you've probably never experienced! It's my desire that you see Jesus in brand-new ways as you uncover important aspects about your spiritual life.

So thanks for coming along for the ride. (And by the way, where's your seatbelt? You're going to need it. Using your imagination will be quite an adventure!)

How to Use This Book as an Individual:

1. Look through this book for a Guided Meditation that sounds interesting. You don't have to start at the beginning.
2. Find a comfortable place where you feel relaxed. Take a deep breath, and then exhale slowly, allowing the cares of your day to disappear for a while. Pray and invite God to join you in this adventure.
3. Slowly read through the Guided Meditation or listen carefully as it's read on the accompanying audio CD. As you do, use your imagination and enter into the story.
4. Next, take a few minutes to journal about what you experienced from the meditation. (Note: See the sidebar on what journaling is, and how it's done.)
5. Take some time to read the accompanying Scripture reference(s) or listen carefully as Scripture is read on the accompanying audio CD.
6. Then take some time to answer the Questions for Reflection. (Feel free to write your answers and any other insights underneath each Question for Reflection—and even in the margins as well as in your own journal. Make this a book you're not afraid to mark up with your thoughts!)
7. Share your experience with some good friends. Have them give it a try!

How to Use This Book with a Group:

1. Look through this book and find a Guided Meditation that you think will appeal to your particular group. Provide pens and paper (or group members can use their own journals if they have them).

2. Ask those in your group to get into comfortable, relaxed positions. Encourage them to take deep breaths and slowly exhale. Invite them to close their eyes if this helps them concentrate better.

3. Now invite them to listen to the Guided Meditation as you read it out loud or play it for them from the audio CD. Challenge them to use their imaginations and enter into the story.

4. After the reading, ask group members to take some time to journal about what they experienced. (Note: See the section below on what journaling is, and how it's done.)

Journaling Defined (adapted from Ken Gire's book, *The Reflective Life*):

"Keeping a regular written record of occurrences, experiences, and reflections of your life for the purpose of spiritual enrichment."

The question is not what you look at, but what you see.
—Henry David Thoreau

BENEFITS OF KEEPING A JOURNAL

Journaling:

• Opens a dialogue with God about life.

• Helps you better understand who you are, where you've been, where you're going, and what's driving you there.

• Helps you develop as a human "being" instead of as a human "doing."

• Gives you an opportunity to slow down from the hurried pace of life.

• Is an activity where God can show up in unbelievable ways!

HOW TO START JOURNALING...

You can invest in a nice leather-bound journal from a local bookstore or simply begin your journaling experience with a cheap spiral-bound notebook. I suggest you invest in a nicer

journal because this is going to be something you'll want to review years from now. Many men and women of faith use the spiritual exercise of journaling to help them deepen their relationships with God. So even if you've never tried it before, why not give it a shot?

• Take your journal, a pen or pencil, and your Bible to a quiet place where you can spend some uninterrupted time alone with God.

• Begin with a simple prayer. Something like this: "God, I've come here to spend some time with you. Please meet me here and help me as I try to express in writing what's on my mind and in my soul."

• If it helps to get your thoughts flowing, open your Bible and read a passage of Scripture, or you can simply open your journal and jump in.

The following are some suggested journal-entry ideas. Don't feel the need to fill the page with writing. Write as much or as little as you feel God leading you to write. Then spend a few minutes reading through your entry when you're done.

• Write your own prayer to God.

• Write a letter to God expressing how you feel about him, telling God something you're thankful for or asking questions.

• Write a letter from God to you. What would God say to you about the way you're living your life today?

• Simply write out how you're feeling in relationship to God and the spiritual life.

• Make up some of your own poetry to express yourself.

• Go beyond words by drawing or doodling your thoughts to God.

5. Next, read the Scripture reference(s) included with the Guided Meditation (or listen carefully as Scripture is read on the accompanying audio CD) and get the group's reaction to a few of

the Questions for Reflection. This will be a great place to start a spiritual discussion with your group.

6. When you believe the conversation has run its course, be sure to ask for volunteers to read their journal entries aloud to the group.

7. Spend a few minutes in prayer as a group thanking God for giving you imaginations and for meeting you in this exercise.

8. Encourage students to try a few Guided Meditation exercises on their own.

How to Get the Most from the Audio CD

It's often helpful to listen to another person read meditations or Scriptures so you can close your eyes and more easily let your imagination carry you into the narrative. So this book comes with an audio CD containing a selection of 15 narrated meditations from this book that you can use when you want to let someone else "tell you the story."

Within each meditation track are two sub-tracks: 1) A reading of the meditation over music (the music fades to silence with enough time between sub-tracks to pause playback for journaling); 2) A reading of accompanying Bible passages over music (the music fades to silence with enough time before end of track to pause before the start of the next meditation track).

CD TRACK LIST:

1. The Celebration	9. In the Still of the Night
2. A Lonely Walk	10. The First Snow
3. What a Place!	11. Talk to Me
4. Saying Goodbye	12. Today Is the Day
5. Behind the Mask	13. Living in a Material World
6. The Most Painful Place	14. Dreaming Big Dreams
7. Taking Inventory	15. Forgiving the Unforgivable
8. The Struggle	

I love baseball. I practically grew up playing the game with my dad and brother. I even played in high school and college. But there's one aspect of the game I've always hated: Practice!

You've heard the saying, "Practice makes perfect." My dad used to tell me that almost every day. I got sick of hearing it. I was really sick of that saying on those cold December mornings when my high school coach took the pitchers and catchers out running to help us develop our leg strength. Coach told us that our strength during the season would only be as strong as our legs, and so we needed to push ourselves beyond our limits if we wanted to be the best. Man, I hated that!

Maybe I hated it because of the way it made my body feel after the first few practice sessions: I ached all over. It seemed like all we ever did was run around the gym and then up and down the stairways. Then we did some weight lifting, a ton of infield drills, and…you guessed it… more running thrown in before practice was over. I always thought it was a huge waste of time. I wanted to get out on the field. I wanted to play the game. I wanted to be on the mound in the final inning with runners on base and my back up against the wall. I loved playing the games, but I hated practice.

That is, until an eventful confrontation with my coach that went something like this:

Coach: You have the potential to be one of the better pitchers on this team, but you refuse to push yourself. You don't practice as hard as the other guys. You're lazy.

He had my attention.

Coach: You think we push you guys like this in practice for no reason? Do you think I get up early and go running with you every morning for my own health?

Me: Well, *yeah!*

Coach: We push you because we want you to be the best you can possibly be. We push you because we see something in you that you may not even see. So, do you want it or not?

I was stunned. I never thought about practice that way before. I did want to be the best I could be! So I dedicated myself to training hard. I started showing up early for weightlifting. I ran the extra lap at the end of practice. I pushed myself up and down those stairs until my legs couldn't take it anymore. And guess what happened? My performance improved. It really did. I would've never believed it before I decided to go for it, but I started to see a difference in my game. And that made me want to practice even harder!

What would you think if I told you that our spiritual life works the same way? It does. But why don't many Christians think of it that way? For some reason, a lot of well-intentioned Christians seem to believe that the important work is over once they've made a commitment to follow Jesus. But following someone is not a passive act. Following Jesus means learning from him and allowing him to teach you how to live your life. Following Jesus means developing spiritual "exercises" in your spiritual life that'll give your soul a workout and help you become a better follower.

When my baseball coach pushed me in practice, he used specific drills and exercises. They were the same drills and exercises that coaches have used for decades to develop young, immature baseball players into solid, seasoned athletes. Again, the spiritual life is no different. There are specific spiritual exercises people have used through the years to develop young, immature followers of Christ into the kind of people God created them to be from the beginning. So why don't we use these same spiritual practices today? Have we forgotten about them? Have they lost their effectiveness? Or have we just gotten lazy?

In his magnificent book, *The Divine Conspiracy: Rediscovering Our Hidden Life in God*, author Dallas Willard talks about the importance of these spiritual practices (he calls them "spiritual disciplines") and the role they should play in our lives if we want to become more like Jesus. Willard defines spiritual disciplines as "any activity within our power that we engage in to enable us to do what we cannot do by direct effort" (353). According to this definition, just about anything can be a spiritual discipline!

Look at it like this: When I was learning how to hit a baseball, my dad went to the store and bought me a batting tee. He didn't start pitching to me right away. He used the tee to help me develop a level swing. When I practiced my swing as a high school player, I often pulled out a batting tee and took 50 swings off the tee to be sure my swing was level. Practicing with the batting tee became a discipline for me.

In the spiritual life, there are several time-tested disciplines that we can use to become more like Jesus himself. One of them—meditation—we learned about in the previous section and is a *huge* part of this book. Now let's take a closer look at some others.

Spiritual Practices for Becoming More Like Jesus

1. **Solitude and Silence:** These two spiritual practices are linked together in Scripture because of the powerful effect of their combination.

   Solitude means to be alone for long periods of time, to be out of contact with other human beings. Jesus modeled the importance of this particular spiritual practice throughout the New Testament by regularly pulling away by himself to rest, be alone, and recharge his soul (Luke 5:16). The great Christian philosopher Blaise Pascal once said, "I have discovered that all the unhappiness of men arises from one single fact, that they are unable to stay quietly in their own room" (*Pascal Selections*, 214).

   Silence means simply the absence of sound. To be silent means to be quiet and listen. Many people are scared of silence because they're afraid of what they might hear God say to them if they settle down and do nothing. But there's nothing to be afraid of. Although it may seem awkward at first, if we learn to set aside regular times in our day to get alone and be quiet with God, we'll hear him whisper wonderful words of encouragement as we travel in our spiritual journey. Give it a try! Start with 10 minutes and work your way up to an amount of time that seems right to you. Try to simply be alone and listen to God. Someone once said that until we teach ourselves to be alone with God, we will never truly be able to be with other people. How do you think silence and solitude can help us develop this important aspect of our spiritual lives?

2. **Fasting:** The biblical practice of fasting involves abstaining from eating for a short period of time. It could also mean refraining from doing something you enjoy or consider important. The hunger you experience during a food fast, for instance, reminds you of what you're striving for spiritually—and can help you get there. You also use the time you would normally spend eating, playing video games, watching TV—or whatever else you're fasting from—to spend time with God. But it's better to not go out of your way to show what you're doing—in Matthew 6:16-18, Jesus makes it clear that you shouldn't fast from food or anything else simply to impress people with how self-disciplined and "holy" you are. Fasting is an act of worship to God and God only!

Warning: Make sure to check with your parents, youth pastor, and your family doctor before practicing any fast involving food! Remember: Fasting is a spiritual discipline, meant to be temporary, and is most definitely not a weight-loss method.

3. **Bible Reading and Memorization:** Even if you're not very good at memorizing certain things, it's a great spiritual practice to write down sections of Scripture on note cards and carry them with you throughout the day. Getting God's Word into our minds and our souls helps change the way we live. I once heard someone I highly respect say, "If I were forced to practice only one spiritual discipline, it would be Bible memorization because of the spiritual power it has unleashed in my own life."

It's important to remember that the Bible is actually a living document that has the power to transform our lives (Hebrews 4:12). God's Word is powerful and effective (2 Timothy 3:16). It has the ability to speak to us when we approach it with the right motivation. Check out Deuteronomy 17:18-19 to see how much God wanted Old Testament kings to undertake this practice of copying Scripture: "When he takes the throne of his kingdom, he is to write for himself on a scroll a copy of this law, taken from that of the priests, who are Levites. It is to be with him, and he is to read it all the days of his life so that he may learn to revere the LORD his God and follow carefully all the words of this law and these decrees."

4. **Spiritual Journaling:** Growing up, I heard some girls I knew talk about writing in their diaries and reading each other's diaries. I thought it was all pretty weird. So several years ago when a friend of mine suggested I do some spiritual journaling, I was less than enthusiastic. *Journaling's for girls!* I told myself. *Why would any guy in his right mind want anything to do with it?* But I guess my friend read my mind, because the next thing he did was tell me about some of the great men of faith down through the years and how every single one of them practiced spiritual journaling. Notable Christians like C.S. Lewis and D.L. Moody. (I also wondered if being good at spiritual journaling meant being known by two initials instead of a real first name! Once my friend assured me that I didn't, I started experimenting with this spiritual practice.)

At first it was awkward. What was I supposed to write about? And who was I writing to, anyway? It was all very confusing. So I stopped and prayed. I simply asked God to meet me where I was and guide my thoughts as I wrote. It was pretty tough at first, but after I stopped worrying about finding the right words, I started writing what was on my mind. I was worried about school and some of the challenges I was facing. I wrote to God about it. I was struggling in a relationship with a friend. I wrote down some thoughts that were very helpful to me when I went back and later read what I had written. The more I wrote, the more comfortable I felt about it.

Spiritual journaling differs from simply keeping a diary in that you intentionally focus your writing on how it relates to God and your spiritual life. Writing down prayers or asking God for direction on something you're facing is a great place to start. And don't be afraid to diagram things in your journal or even use some of your artistic ability to express yourself to God. Question yourself in your journal, too, then go back and read your words later. If you're like me, you'll probably be surprised at something you wrote. It may even prove helpful as you journey down the spiritual path God has you on.

Your journal is a great barometer of what's going on in your heart. When you make spiritual journaling a regular exercise in your life, you'll be amazed at how often God shows up and meets you right where you are. (And since journaling is a significant part of this book, by reading these pages you'll get a great head start with this important exercise!)

5. **Prayer:** Prayer is a simple conversation with God—the one who created you and loves you. A conversation involves both talking and listening. This is important to realize when you're praying. God isn't impressed with lots of words or flowery language. God just wants to spend time hanging out with you and listening to what's on your heart.

Is it difficult for you to have a conversation with your best friend? Do you have to think carefully about what you're going to say when you're around people you love? Do your friends at school expect you to speak a certain way when you're hanging out together and having fun? Of course not! When you're around people who love you, it should be easy to be yourself, right? Then why do so many people have such a difficult time having a conversation with God?

I don't know about you, but sometimes it's hard for me to get started when I'm trying to pray. I don't know whether it's because I'm easily distracted, or because I can't actually see God, or because I'm so tired at times when I'm trying to pray that I fall asleep. But at times I find it tough to pray. So I've recently started using some prayer "helpers" to keep me focused as I pray. Some of those helpers include:

- Walking while I pray
- Praying with my eyes open
- Reciting The Lord's Prayer as I get started
- Praying The Jesus Prayer several times ("Jesus Christ, Son of God, have mercy on me, a sinner. Amen.")

People connect with God in many different ways. Pick one of these prayer helpers and give it a try. This is a spiritual exercise worth developing in your life. Prayer has power. Prayer changes things. So spend some time talking with God and listening for him to speak to you right now. Simply jump in and start talking!

6. **Worship:** We all get different images in our minds when we hear this word. For some, worship is something you "do" on a Sunday morning in church. It usually involves music and singing before someone gets up and preaches. For some, this is a meaningful and spiritual experience. Others spend more time counting the number of holes in the ceiling tiles than anything else. To them, the worship service is about as compelling as a lecture on the history of socks. But is worship something that only happens in a church service on a Sunday morning? Or is it something completely different?

Worship can happen on a Sunday morning in church—and it can also happen every other day of the week as we go about our lives. As we express our gratitude to God for doing so much for us and *just being God*, we learn to worship God in everything we say and do. Worship is an important spiritual exercise worth developing because it reminds us that there is a God—and we are not him. It helps gives us a proper perspective of our lives.

According to most dictionaries, *worship* means "worth-ship." Worship happens when you express how valuable something or someone is to you. True worship is an invaluable spiritual exercise that we would all do well to develop in our lives.

If God is important to you (i.e., "valuable" to you), how do you express worship to God? What are some ways to let God know that? You could sing to God. You could pray and express yourself. And, most importantly, according to Scripture, you could gather with other Christ-followers and express your worship to God. ("Let us not give up meeting together, as some are in the habit of doing, but let us encourage one another—and all the more as you see the Day approaching." Hebrews 10:25)

Solitude, silence, fasting, Bible reading and memorization, spiritual journaling, prayer, and worship. These—along with meditation—are some of the important spiritual practices that all Christ-followers should consider. When we learn how to use them in our everyday lives, they help us become more and more like Jesus himself.

Again, this book is all about helping you "chew upon" spiritual things in your life. It's intended to get you thinking about your relationship with God and to challenge you to become more and more like his Son, Jesus Christ, by paying attention to all of the various senses God gave you—and by using your imagination!

One More Time!
A Word about Following Our Guide...the Holy Spirit

I have good news for you: As we head out on this spiritual journey together, we're not going alone. Most likely some of you reading this book aren't familiar with Guided Meditations and how they work. It may be reassuring for you to know that as we venture into the world of Guided Meditations, we have an actual Guide to help us along the way—the Holy Spirit.

The Bible says that after Jesus died on the cross and rose from the dead, he ascended into heaven and sat at the place of highest honor at God the Father's right hand. But here's some more great news: While Jesus left the earth and his followers, he didn't leave us here all by ourselves. He didn't abandon us. Not only did he promise to return to earth someday and take us back to heaven with him forever, but also he left his Holy Spirit to guide us as we walk our spiritual journeys. God's Holy Spirit enables us to meditate on Scripture and actually experience and have a relationship with Jesus.

In the Gospel of John, Jesus tells his disciples that he'll soon be leaving them. The disciples are confused. They thought he was going to be their leader and king—the one who would save them from the oppression of the Roman government. So they're anxious to know who will lead them once Jesus leaves. This is where Jesus teaches them about a friend he'll send to them. This friend will guide the disciples along their spiritual journeys and direct them back to what Jesus taught them in the first place. This "friend" is God's Holy Spirit, who always directs God's followers to Jesus and his teachings. In John 16:13, Jesus says his Holy Spirit will guide them into all truth and will speak only what he hears from the Father.

So how does God's Holy Spirit guide us today? Through the Bible, through events and circumstances in our lives, through prayer, through dreams, through other people, and probably many other ways, as well. But one of the most important ways God's Spirit speaks to us is through the imagination. For whatever reason, many people don't pay much attention to the power of their imaginations. Yet God uses this special part of us in powerful ways.

When we tap into our imaginations, we can unplug from the noise of the world and enjoy a quiet moment with God. We can slow down and use our minds to focus on God. Even Albert Einstein understood the power we so often keep locked away in the recesses of our minds when he said, "Imagination is more important than knowledge."

Some people get freaked out about imagination. Maybe they're afraid of how wildly creative their own imaginations can be. But here's something important to remember from John 16:13. God's Spirit will never say anything that goes beyond or contradicts what God has already said to us through the Bible. God is a God of communication. God doesn't want to keep things hidden from us. We want to know; God wants to tell us. Maybe not right away, but at just the right time, God will always lead us in truth closer to him. And God certainly does use our imaginations to communicate with us.

Guided Meditations are a way of paying attention to what God wants to say to us. The meditations in this book are intended to engage different memories and experiences you've had in your life so you see God in the midst of it all. You have some incredible stories locked away inside of you. You simply need to tap into them to hear God's voice.

As you prepare to experience God's Spirit personally through these Guided Meditations, understand that none of us has the power to command God to show up and speak whenever and wherever we want. But as we slow down, take a deep breath, relax, and get in touch with our own imaginations, we may hear God whispering to us. Undoubtedly that whisper will sound something like this: "I love you. I'm crazy about you! I can't wait to be near you and hang out with you."

So find a comfortable spot, take a few deep breaths, and relax. Ready? Then let's jump in together!

The Celebration

Chapter 1

Guided Meditation

Imagine yourself sitting at a table surrounded by people you know very well. All eyes seem to be on you. Who's sitting at the table with you? Are any of your family members there? Which of your friends are seated at the table? A sense of anticipation fills the room. Everyone is waiting for the special moment. How are you feeling? What's going through your mind as everyone is watching you?

Suddenly the lights go out and the doors fly open. Someone is walking toward the table with a cake. Candles are burning on top of it. It's for you. It's your birthday cake! Everyone begins singing, "Happy birthday to you…happy birthday to you." What's going through your mind as everyone sings to you? Why do you imagine these particular people at the table with you? Is anyone missing who should be here?

As everyone finishes singing, someone asks you to make a wish. What do you wish for? What if your wish could come true? How would it change things? Or would it? As you close your eyes to blow out the candles, what are you thinking about? What's your heart telling you? As the smoke from the candles begins to clear and the lights go on again, it seems as though everyone is waiting for you to say something. What happens next?

Journal Entry

_____

_____

_____

_____

_____

_____

_____

_____

_____

_____

Scripture Guides Us

The Bible describes the day of your birth as a significant event. God celebrates your birthday because you are created in his image, and God wants a relationship with you forever. God celebrates your life because you're created to experience the fullness of the incredible life God's given you.

Take a few minutes to "chew on" the following Scripture verses, allowing God's Spirit to speak to you.

PSALM 139:13-16

For you created my inmost being; you knit me together in my mother's womb. I praise you because I am fearfully and wonderfully made; your works are wonderful, I know that full well. My frame was not hidden from you when I was made in the secret place. When I was woven together in the depths of the earth, your eyes saw my unformed body. All the days ordained for me were written in your book before one of them came to be.

JOHN 10:10

"The thief comes only to steal and kill and destroy; I have come that they may have life, and have it to the full."

EPHESIANS 2:10

For we are God's handiwork, created in Christ Jesus to do good works, which God prepared in advance for us to do.

Questions for Reflection

1. Why do you think God is so up on life?

2. What makes you feel fully alive?

3. What do you think it means to be God's "workmanship"?

4. If you could choose only three people to be at the table with you, who would they be? Why?

5. Which of your birthday celebrations brings back the best memories? Why?

6. Which birthday celebration, if any, would you rather not remember? Why not?

7. What would your life be like if God gave you everything you wished for? What are you wishing for most in life right now? Why?

8. How can unfulfilled wishes sometimes be a blessing in disguise?

9. What would you say to the people at the table if you had the chance?

10. Do you ever feel obligated to say something when you wish you could just stay quiet? How does that make you feel?

11. What do you think Jesus would say to you if he were sitting at the table with you on your birthday? What would you say to him if you could?

The Big Day

Chapter 2

Guided Meditation

There's something different about your house today. As you walk from room to room, you notice piles of boxes stacked up everywhere. Some of them are all taped up and have writing on the sides. Others are still open and some things are still waiting to be packed into them. Newspaper is scattered everywhere and you can tell that moving day is fast approaching. As you head down the hallway leading to your bedroom, all kinds of memories from your childhood begin to flood your mind. Which memories stand out? Why do you think you remember these so vividly?

As you walk into your room, you notice most of your possessions stacked in boxes and leaning against the wall. How does it make you feel to see everything you own in one place like this? You notice a few more boxes that still need to be packed. What do you want to make sure gets in there? What if you weren't able to take a few of your things because there wasn't enough room? What would you leave behind if you absolutely had to? Why do you think you would choose those things rather than something else?

Once you finish packing the last few things from your room into boxes, you start to imagine what your new life is going to look like. What will your new house be like? What about your new room? How do you imagine it? How will you arrange your things? What do you imagine your new life being like? Do you think it will be hard to make new friends or fit in?

As you lean back against the boxes to think some more, someone walks into your room and sits down next to you. What happens next?

Journal Entry

_____

_____

_____

_____

_____

_____

_____

_____

_____

_____

Scripture Guides Us

The Bible never mentions anything about Jesus owning a home—or any property for that matter. He seems totally dependent upon others to supply his needs as he travels from town to town sharing the Good News of God. What faith he must have had in his heavenly Father to take care of him!

Take a few minutes to "chew on" the following Scripture verses, allowing God's Spirit to speak to you.

LUKE 9:57-58

As they were walking along the road, a man said to him, "I will follow you wherever you go." Jesus replied, "Foxes have holes and birds have nests, but the Son of Man has no place to lay his head."

Questions for Reflection

1. What do you think Jesus meant when he said, "But the Son of Man has no place to lay his head"?

2. Describe how you would feel if you found out you had to move to a different state in the next few weeks?

3. What do you think the most difficult part of moving would be?

4. What would the best part of moving be?

5. What are your three biggest memories from childhood and growing up where you did?

6. What would you miss most if you were unable to take it with you? Why?

7. If you were moving to a completely different part of the country, which friends would you miss the most? Why?

8. How does what you own tell someone about who you are?

9. Who do you imagine came into your room at the end to talk with you? What did this person have to say?

A Lonely Walk

Chapter 3

Guided Meditation

Imagine yourself walking along a path into the woods. As you continue to walk, the path seems to be getting deeper and darker. You're not as familiar with your surroundings as when you began this journey, and the darkness seems to be settling in by the minute. What are you going to do? Are you getting tired? Are you getting hot? Are you feeling cold? Are you sweating or shivering? What does the path ahead of you look like?

You feel the weight of your backpack on your back so you stop for a minute to take it off and rest. As you look through it, what do you see? What did you bring with you on this trip?

As you sit by the edge of the trail, you hear something stirring in the woods, coming toward you on the path up ahead. You can't quite see anything yet, but you definitely hear footsteps. As you stand up and put the backpack on again, now you can see who it is coming toward you on the path ahead. It's Jesus!

As you meet on the path, he looks you right in the eyes. Neither of you says a word. What do you suppose he's thinking about as he stares at you? After a few more seconds, he asks to carry your backpack for you. How does his request make you feel? What do you say? You notice

Jesus is already carrying a few other backpacks. Who do they belong to? What do you think is in them? As you turn and walk along together, it seems as if Jesus knows exactly where he's going and it's almost as if he's leading you now. What do you say to each other as you walk along?

Journal Entry

_____

_____

_____

_____

_____

_____

_____

_____

_____

Scripture Guides Us

There's nowhere you can go where God can't find you. You are never really lost from God's point of view. God will continue to run after you until you allow God to "find" you and begin enjoying a relationship with him.

Take a few minutes to "chew on" the following Scripture verses, allowing God's Spirit to speak to you.

JOHN 9:35-38

Jesus heard that they had thrown him out, and when he found him, he said, "Do you believe in the Son of Man?" "Who is he, sir?" the man asked. "Tell me so that I may believe in him." Jesus said, "You have now seen him; in fact, he is the one speaking with you." Then the man said, "Lord, I believe," and he worshiped him.

Questions for Reflection

1. Describe a time in your life when you tried to run away from God.

2. Have you ever experienced being found by God like the man in John 9? How did that make you feel?

3. What do you think you were doing in the woods in the first place? Why were you all alone?

4. Have you ever experienced what it feels like to be lost? How did it make you feel? What did you do?

5. What was in your backpack? What do you think is the significance of those items?

Chew on This

6. How did it make you feel when you heard the rustling noise in the woods? What did you think it was at first?

7. How did you feel when you first saw Jesus coming toward you on the path?

8. Why do you think Jesus looked you in the eyes so deeply? What do you suppose he was thinking about you?

9. Why do you think Jesus asked to carry your backpack? Did you let him? Was that decision easy for you? Why or why not?

10. What was important about the other backpacks Jesus was carrying?

11. How did it make you feel to follow Jesus?

12. Where do you think Jesus was taking you? What were you going to do once you arrived?

Christmas Morning

Chapter 4

Guided Meditation

As you come into the room where your Christmas tree is, the first thing you notice are all of the presents under the tree. Even the Christmas stockings hung by the chimney have gifts bulging out of them! You can hardly wait for the rest of your family to wake up so you can start opening your presents. But for now, there's a quiet stillness in the house that you've never noticed before.

As you walk toward the Christmas tree, you notice that a few of Santa's cookies are missing, along with the glass of milk you left for him the night before. You smile as you remember believing in Santa when you were much younger. On the same table as Santa's cookies stands the nativity scene your family puts out every Christmas season. You stop to look at it a little more closely and your imagination begins to take you back to that moment in time. You wonder what it would have been like to be Mary giving birth in a stable. There are many things you wonder about that baby.

Eventually you head over to the Christmas tree and you notice a couple of presents with your name on them. You pick one up and shake it gently, trying to figure out what might be inside. You notice all of the unique ornaments on the tree and remember the stories your parents have told you about each one as you helped them decorate the tree.

"What's the meaning behind all of this?" you wonder. "Why do we go through all of this every year?" As your mind drifts in thought, you hear the sounds of your family beginning to wake up and head toward you, so you quickly put your present back under the tree. You're ready to wish everyone a Merry Christmas.

Journal Entry

_____

_____

_____

_____

_____

_____

_____

_____

_____

_____

Scripture Guides Us

Our God is a God of mystery and intrigue. Just when we think we've got God figured out, God surprises us.

Take a few minutes to "chew on" the following Scripture verses, allowing God's Spirit to speak to you.

MATTHEW 7:11

"If you, then, though you are evil, know how to give good gifts to your children, how much more will your Father in heaven give good gifts to those who ask him!"

LUKE 2:6-14

While they were there, the time came for the baby to be born, and she gave birth to her firstborn, a son. She wrapped him in cloths and placed him in a manger, because there was no guest room available for them. And there were shepherds living out in the fields nearby, keeping watch over their flocks at night. An angel of the Lord appeared to them, and the glory of the Lord shone around them, and they were terrified. But the angel said to them, "Do not be afraid. I bring you good news of great joy that will be for all the people. Today in the town of David a Savior has been born to you; he is Messiah, the Lord. This will be a sign to you: You will find a baby wrapped in cloths and lying in a manger." Suddenly a great company of the heavenly host appeared with the angel, praising God and saying, "Glory to God in the highest heaven, and on earth peace to those on whom his favor rests."

Questions for Reflection

1. What Christmas rituals does your family have?

2. What different emotions stir inside your soul by thinking about Christmas? Why do you think that is?

3. What was the best gift you ever received at Christmas? Why?

Chew on This

4. What was the best gift you ever gave to someone at Christmas? Why?

5. How would you have felt if you had never opened your gifts under the tree that day?

6. How does it make you feel to be able to give good gifts?

7. Describe how you would have felt if you were Mary or Joseph dealing with an illegitimate baby and all of the shame that went with it in that culture.

8. Why do you think God chose to come to earth like he did?

What a Place!

Chapter 5

Guided Meditation

An unexplainable sense of peace overwhelms you as you begin exploring your new digs. Everything is bright and airy. You're seeing colors that you've never seen, hearing sounds you've never heard, and feeling things in a brand-new way—unlike anything you've ever experienced. All of your senses seem more alive than ever.

Suddenly you catch a whiff of something that you've never smelled before. It smells so good! As you walk over to see what it is, you notice that someone has prepared all of your favorite foods. You see them all beautifully displayed on a long table right before your very eyes.

Then you hear a voice coming from the head of the table inviting you to sit down and eat. You can't see who it is because it's so bright at the end of the table. You sit down. Then you notice some other people coming to eat with you; they're some of your favorite people ever! As they gather around you at the table, they begin engaging you in conversation.

All of a sudden it hits you—you're in heaven! All of these people at the table with you are friends and relatives who've already passed on. Your thoughts are interrupted as the person at the head of the table stands to welcome you, and everyone else says how happy they are that you've come. You feel full of joy and more alive than you've ever felt. You feel like you're finally home.

Journal Entry

_____

_____

_____

_____

_____

_____

_____

_____

_____

_____

Scripture Guides Us

How can we ever begin to understand what heaven might be like when we've never experienced anything even close to it?

Take a few minutes to "chew on" the following Scripture verse, allowing God's Spirit to speak to you.

REVELATION 19:9

Then the angel said to me, "Write: 'Blessed are those who are invited to the wedding supper of the Lamb!'" And he added, "These are the true words of God."

Questions for Reflection

1. What have you pictured heaven being like? Why? How does the guided meditation match up to your expectations?

2. What foods were prepared for you on the table? Seeing all of your favorite foods on this table, it's almost as though the person preparing it knew you. How does that make you feel?

3. Who were some of the people with you at the table? Who was missing? Why?

43

4. Who do you think was sitting at the head of the table? Why? How does it make you feel to be eating with this person?

5. Are there any questions you want to ask this person?

6. Why do you think you feel more alive than ever before?

Saying Goodbye

Chapter 6

Guided Meditation

The room is very quiet. The people in it are whispering. You recognize almost everyone in the room, but you're wondering why they all seem so sad. Several photos of you and your family are displayed in the back of the room, and some people have gathered around. They're pointing at them and smiling. Everyone must be thinking of a special memory.

Several flower arrangements decorate the room, and they smell beautiful. But as you look more closely, you notice most of them are set up near a casket in the front of the room. It's then you realize that you're in a funeral home.

As more and more people enter the room and sign the book by the door, several groups move toward the casket. They're talking so quietly that you can't understand what they're saying. But from the few sentences you're able to decipher, it seems they're talking about you.

Now you see your best friend approaching the casket alone. You can't seem to get your friend's attention. Your friend is crying and kneels down next to the casket. That's when you realize that you're in the casket. Your friend is asking you why you had to die. Why did it have to happen the way it did?

Now your parents approach the casket and grab your hand—but you can't feel anything. You can see them crying. You can hear their voices, but you can't seem to respond. You desperately want to communicate with them, but things seem to be fading away so quickly. It's getting darker in the room. Your senses are beginning to disappear completely. As things are almost completely fading away, you notice your parents bending over to kiss you on the forehead.

Journal Entry

_____

_____

_____

_____

_____

_____

_____

_____

_____

Scripture Guides Us

Death is one of the most difficult things to think about for most people. Most of us are afraid of dying. Why do you think that is? Why is it so hard to talk about, anyway?

Take a few minutes to "chew on" the following Scripture verses, allowing God's Spirit to speak to you.

HEBREWS 9:27

People are destined to die once, and after that to face judgment.

1 CORINTHIANS 15:54-57

"Death has been swallowed up in victory. Where, O death is your victory? Where, O death is your sting?" The sting of death is sin, and the power of sin is the law. But thanks be to God! He gives us the victory through our Lord Jesus Christ.

Questions for Reflection

1. Who are some of the people you imagined visiting at the funeral? Who was missing? Why?

2. What did you feel like when you realized that *you* were the one lying in the casket?

3. What do you think your friends would say about you at your funeral? Why should that matter to you?

4. Describe how you feel about death and the idea of dying someday. How have you experienced death in your life so far?

5. What scares you most about death? Why?

6. What are you doing in this life to prepare yourself for the next one?

7. Why do you think it's so difficult for most people to talk about death?

Help Me!

Chapter 7

Guided Meditation

Your family has been going through some tough times lately. Your dad lost his job. Your mom got sick and is going through a long and difficult recovery. After several months of not being able to pay the bills, you've found yourselves living in a temporary housing shelter. Your dad is doing all he can to provide for your family, but it isn't enough. You're working, too, but your job pays minimum wage and the bill collectors still want more. You never would've imagined this a few years ago, but you now find yourself standing on the median at the end of the freeway off-ramp holding a sign that simply says, "Please help. Tough times." It's raining and cold and a long line of cars fill the off-ramp, waiting for the light to change. You need to collect enough money to buy your family dinner tonight, but no one is giving you the time of day. Most people don't even look at you through their car windows. Some are busy talking on their cell phones; others do a terrible job of pretending not to notice you.

Suddenly a driver beeps her horn. She wants you to come over to her car window before the light changes. As you walk up to her brand-new BMW, she reaches out through the window and hands you some change. "God bless you," she says before quickly rolling her window back up and heading off into the rainy night. As you open up your hand to count the money, you notice she has given you 37 cents and a tract that tells you how to become a Christian. Realizing that the money won't get you very far, you head back to where you were standing before and continue holding your sign. How do you feel as the cars go racing past you? What do you notice about the people staring at you? How do you plan on providing dinner for your family tonight if no one else stops to help you? It's getting colder now and the rain is getting heavier. The traffic has thinned out considerably, so you decide to head back to the shelter for the night.

Journal Entry

_____

_____

_____

_____

_____

_____

_____

_____

_____

Scripture Guides Us

Few of us can imagine what life is like without a home. We've probably all felt a little awkward when we see someone standing on the street asking for money. What should we do? Can we help? Or would we be making things worse if we somehow get involved?

Take a few minutes to "chew on" the following Scripture verses, allowing God's Spirit to speak to you.

HEBREWS 13:1-2

Keep on loving each other as brothers and sisters. Do not forget to show hospitality to strangers, for by so doing some people have shown hospitality to angels without knowing it.

JAMES 2:2-6

Suppose someone comes into your meeting wearing a gold ring and fine clothes, and a poor person in filthy old clothes also comes in. If you show special attention to the one wearing fine clothes and say, "Here's a good seat for you," but say to the one who is poor, "You stand there" or "Sit on the floor by my feet," have you not discriminated among yourselves and become judges with evil thoughts? Listen, my dear brothers and sisters: Has not God chosen those who are poor in the eyes of the world to be rich in faith and to inherit the kingdom he promised those who love him? But you have dishonored the poor.

MATTHEW 26:11

"The poor you will always have with you."

Questions for Reflection

1. How does it make you feel when you see someone on the streets begging for money? Have you ever stopped to help someone like that? Why or why not?

2. How are most homeless people viewed by our culture? What could you do to change that?

3. How do you think you would have reacted toward the woman who gave you 37 cents and a Christian tract?

4. In Matthew 26:11 Jesus said, "The poor you will always have with you." Why do you think it is important for us to have the poor among us?

5. If it were within your power to do something to help the poor in your community, what would you do? What is stopping you from doing it?

6. How could you begin to change the way some of your friends think about the poor in your community?

7. Do you think you could ever become homeless? What do you think you would do?

Repeat After Me

Chapter 8

Guided Meditation

You're in a small room in the back of a church with some of your closest friends. Everyone is more dressed up than you've ever seen them, and they all seem to be centering their attention on you. A few of your family members buzz in and out of the room along with a man taking photographs of everyone.

Suddenly someone bursts into the room and says, "It's time to go! It's time to go!" With that, everyone in your group heads down a hallway and into a large room full of people. They're all staring at you and smiling. You can hear music playing and people singing. That's when you realize this is your wedding day.

The next thing you know, you're standing next to your future spouse, facing a minister who's talking to you both about the importance of what you're about to do and the vows you're ready to take.

As you begin to take it all in, you start thinking about this person standing next to you. You've both dreamed about this day for so long that you can hardly believe it's arrived.

Think about the person you're about to marry. How do you know for sure this is the right person for you? Do you know everything you need to know about each other? How do you see your future playing out together? Where will you live? What will you do for a living? How many children do you want to have together? What do you think the other person is thinking about you? Is it okay to be a little scared about all of it?

Your thoughts are interrupted by the minister asking you to, "Repeat these vows after me." Are you ready to commit yourself to this person for the rest of your life? Are you ready to trust someone other than yourself? Excitedly, you begin to recite your vows as you imagine your future together.

Journal Entry

_____

_____

_____

_____

_____

_____

_____

_____

_____

Scripture Guides Us

Some of us have dreamed about our wedding day since we were very young. Others can't even imagine taking a step like that. Do you think God has set aside a spouse for you?

Take a few minutes to "chew on" the following Scripture verses, allowing God's Spirit to speak to you.

EPHESIANS 5:21

Submit to one another out of reverence for Christ.

GENESIS 2:19-25

Now the LORD God had formed out of the ground all the wild animals and all the birds in the sky. He brought them to the man to see what he would name them; and whatever the man called each living creature, that was its name. So the man gave names to all the livestock, the birds in the sky and all the wild animals. But for Adam no suitable helper was found. So the LORD God caused the man to fall into a deep sleep; and while he was sleeping, he took one of the man's ribs and then closed up the place with flesh. Then the LORD God made a woman from the rib he had taken out of the man, and he brought her to the man. The man said, "This is now bone of my bones and flesh of my flesh; she shall be called 'woman,' for she was taken out of man." For this reason a man will leave his father and mother and be united to his wife, and they will become one flesh. The man and his wife were both naked, and they felt no shame.

HEBREWS 13:4

Marriage should be honored by all, and the marriage bed kept pure, for God will judge the adulterer and all the sexually immoral.

Questions for Reflection

1. As you imagine your wedding day, what kind of person do you see yourself marrying someday?

2. What do you think Ephesians 5:21 means when it says, "Submit to one another out of reverence for Christ?"

3. How could you be praying for your future spouse right now?

4. What does it mean for you to make a vow to someone?

5. According to Malachi 2:14, God is also a witness to the vows you take on your wedding day. What difference should that make to you?

6. As you think about the person you would like to marry someday, what strengths and weaknesses do you imagine this person having? How will those strengths and weaknesses complement your own?

7. God often allows us to marry someone he will use in our lives to make us into the kind of people God wants us to be. With that in mind, what type of person do you imagine God bringing into your life?

Chapter 9

Guided Meditation

The darkness is overwhelming. You're trying to find your way home, and there's no one to help you. It's cold and damp, and no matter which way you turn, you always hit a dead end. As you turn around and try to feel your way out, you sense that you may be walking in circles. You call out for help, but no one answers. The night air seems thicker than ever before. You notice a faint light shining through the darkness, so you begin to hurry toward it—but you slip and fall and hurt your leg. Now, in pain, you force yourself back to your feet and begin slowly walking again. What do you feel under your feet? Can you touch anything with your hands? What is that you smell?

Then you think you hear voices whispering in the darkness off the path to your right. Should you see who it is, or should you stay on the path and keep stumbling toward the light? As you try to decide what to do, you lose your footing again on the wet path and begin slipping and sliding down a bank on the left. By the time you stop sliding, you no longer hear the voices or see the light. You sit on the ground in the cold, rainy darkness. What are you feeling now? What do you think you should do?

As you sit in the darkness and cry, you notice another light in the distance—brighter than the one you saw before—and this light seems to be coming closer to you. You feel yourself getting warmer inside as the light draws closer and closer. Suddenly, you recognize the person holding the light and a smile comes across your face. The light-bearer helps you to your feet and you begin walking together.

Journal Entry

Scripture Guides Us

Many people are afraid of the dark. Few people actually enjoy the darkness. Have you ever been lost in the darkness? How did it make you feel? Do you think God knew where you were? Is there anywhere we can go where God doesn't know where we are?

Take a few minutes to "chew on" the following Scripture verses, allowing God's Spirit to speak to you.

PSALM 139:7-12

Where can I go from your Spirit? Where can I flee from your presence? If I go up to the heavens, you are there; if I make my bed in the depths,

you are there. If I rise on the wings of the dawn, if I settle on the far side of the sea, even there your hand will guide me, your right hand will hold me fast. If I say, "Surely the darkness will hide me and the light become night around me," even the darkness will not be dark to you; the night will shine like the day, for darkness is as light to you.

Questions for Reflection

1. Describe a time in your life when you felt lost.

2. What about being lost is so terrifying?

3. How does it make you feel to know that God always knows where you are and what you're going through?

Chew on This

4. Describe a time in your life when you felt lonely. What did you do about it?

5. Who do you think the light represents? Why?

6. Where do you imagine the light leading you?

Behind the Mask

Chapter 10

Guided Meditation

It's one of your favorite nights of the year. In fact, you can't wait for it to start getting dark outside. As you get ready to go, you notice a few porch lights popping on across the street, and you beg your parents to let you go out with your friends alone. After all, you're old enough now, right?

As you finish buttoning up your costume and slipping on your mask, you grab your empty pillowcase and head out the front door, where you meet your friends. First stop—your neighbor's house and the meanest lady in the neighborhood. You can't even believe you're walking up to her front door, but her light is on, and your friends are pulling you along with them. What are you thinking as you knock on the front door and yell, "Trick or treat?"

As the door creaks open slowly, you notice your neighbor is dressed in a funny clown outfit with a huge smile painted on her face. What are you thinking about her as she drops some candy into your pillowcase? She smiles and says, "I love your costume." You say, "Thanks," and head back down the driveway. What kind of costume are you wearing? What made you choose this one anyway?

As you continue on from house to house, how are you feeling about the entire experience? As the chill of the evening begins settling in, dozens of other kids dressed up in costumes and masks pass you on the sidewalk. You wonder to yourself: "Who am I behind this mask? Does anyone know the real me?"

Finally, you snap out of your deep thoughts as one of your friends calls you to the front porch of a house where no one is home...but they've left a bowl full of candy, and it's time to empty it!

Journal Entry

_____

_____

_____

_____

_____

_____

_____

_____

_____

Scripture Guides Us

We all wear different kinds of masks at one point or another in our lives. Some of these masks are meant to protect us, and some of these masks are meant to hide behind. But we all need people who see who we are behind our masks—the real people we are.

Take a few minutes to "chew on" the following Scripture verses, allowing God's Spirit to speak to you.

MATTHEW 23:13, 15

"Woe to you, teachers of the law and Pharisees, you hypocrites! You shut the door of the kingdom of heaven in people's faces. You yourselves do not enter, nor will you let those enter who are trying to. Woe to you, teachers of the law and Pharisees, you hypocrites! You travel over land and sea to win a single convert, and then you make that convert twice as much a son of hell as you are."

Questions for Reflection

1. What kind of mask were you wearing while you were out trick or treating?

2. What kinds of masks do you sometimes hide behind in your everyday life? Why?

3. Who gets to see the real you? Why this person? What makes you trust this person?

4. Why do you think Jesus uses the kind of language he uses when addressing the religious leaders of his day?

5. Are there people in your life you've judged only by outward appearances? What do you think you should do about that?

Floating

Chapter 11

Guided Meditation

It's been a while since you've been on the lake. As the morning mist begins to fade away, you push off the dock and head out. As you stretch back to set the oars in the water, what's going through your mind? Are you excited about spending some time alone with God, or does it scare you? What jumps out at you on this particular morning is how quiet it is on the lake. A few birds chirp from the trees on the banks, but besides that, the only sound you hear is your oars as you row toward the middle of the lake.

You can feel yourself huffing and puffing as you reach your destination and pull the oars into the boat. As you lean back to rest a bit, you feel your heart beating through your chest. What are you thinking about? What have you come here for, anyway? The only sound you hear now is the water rippling against the sides of your boat. It's been a while since you've experienced quiet like this.

As you sit motionless in the boat, you could swear you hear someone calling your name from behind you on the lake. As you turn to see who it is, you can't believe your eyes; it looks as if Jesus is walking on the water toward your boat like he did in the New Testament!

He seems to want you to come toward him. But as you grab the oars to put them back in the water and row to him, Jesus makes it clear that he wants you to have faith and walk toward him on top of the water. What's your initial reaction to what you hear Jesus asking you to do? What do you think you'll do? A surge of excitement wells up inside of you. Part of you can't believe this is actually happening…and part of you is scared to death.

Journal Entry

_____

_____

_____

_____

_____

_____

_____

_____

_____

_____

Scripture Guides Us

Taking a step of faith into anything is a huge challenge for many people. We tend to enjoy the parts of our lives that are safe. But what would happen if we discovered that the safest place ever is right where God wants us to be? Would you be able to take that step of faith even if it meant not knowing what the future might hold?

Take a few minutes to "chew on" the following Scripture verses, allowing God's Spirit to speak to you.

MATTHEW 14:25-33

Shortly before dawn Jesus went out to them, walking on the lake. When the disciples saw him walking on the lake, they were terrified. "It's a ghost," they said, and cried out in fear. But Jesus immediately said to them: "Take courage! It is I. Don't be afraid." "Lord, if it's you," Peter replied, "tell me to come to you on the water." "Come," he said. Then Peter got down out of the boat, walked on the water and came toward Jesus. But when he saw the wind, he was afraid and, beginning to sink, cried out, "Lord, save me!" Immediately Jesus reached out his hand and caught him. "You of little faith," he said, "why did you doubt?" And when they climbed into the boat, the wind died down. Then those who were in the boat worshiped him, saying, "Truly you are the Son of God."

QUESTIONS FOR REFLECTION

1. What do you think is going on in Peter's mind as he takes his first step on the water toward Jesus?

2. Why do you think Peter starts sinking?

3. What do you imagine Jesus is thinking about Peter when he has to keep him from drowning?

4. What do you think would keep you from stepping out on the lake and walking toward Jesus?

5. When is the last time you spent some quiet time alone with God? What keeps you from spending more time with him?

6. Where do you personally need to exercise more faith in your life today? What could you do about it?

The Most Painful Place

Chapter 12

Guided Meditation

It's a normal morning like any other morning, but today you find yourself lying awake in your bed even before your alarm has sounded. As you lie there, nice and cozy under your covers, you feel yourself becoming more and more anxious over the thought of getting up and going to school today. If today is anything like yesterday or the day before that, or even the day before that, you can barely even stomach the thought of returning to school for an entire year!

School seems like the most challenging place in your life right now. It's not the homework or the grades or even your teachers. It's the other students. It's what happens in the hallways between classes and what goes on before and after school on most days.

Students label each other. It's been going on forever. Students put each other in certain categories without even knowing each other very well. Students are made fun of for what they wear, how they look, how they talk, how fat they are, how skinny they are. They're labeled because they have glasses, because they have money, because they're athletic, or because they aren't athletic. They're judged and made fun of because of the color of their skin, their nationality, their religion. They're pushed around and made into the butt of one joke after another. (Oh well, it's only a joke, right? When has a joke hurt anybody, anyway?)

As you lie there in the stillness of the morning before your alarm sounds, you catch yourself thinking about this school that you're a part of. Is it everything you want it to be? Are you proud of yourself? Your classmates?

Journal Entry

_____

_____

_____

_____

_____

_____

_____

_____

_____

_____

Scripture Guides Us

It's amazing how powerful words can be. The things we say to and about other people carry a lot of weight. We can use our words to hurt people, and we can use our words to help people. How important is it for us to think about our words before we speak them?

Take a few minutes to "chew on" the following Scripture verses, allowing God's Spirit to speak to you.

EPHESIANS 4:29

Do not let any unwholesome talk come out of your mouths, but only what is helpful for building others up according to their needs, that it may benefit those who listen.

MATTHEW 15:18

"But the things that come out of the mouth come from the heart."

PHILIPPIANS 4:6-8

Do not be anxious about anything, but in every situation, by prayer and petition, with thanksgiving, present your requests to God. And the peace of God, which transcends all understanding, will guard your hearts and your minds in Christ Jesus. Finally, brothers and sisters, whatever is true, whatever is noble, whatever is right, whatever is pure, whatever is lovely, whatever is admirable—if anything is excellent or praiseworthy—think about such things.

Questions for Reflection

1. Have you ever been hurt by another person's joking around? How did it make you feel? Is there anything you wished you would've done differently?

2. Which side of this are you on? Are you the one being labeled and judged? Or are you doing the labeling and judging most of the time? How does that make you feel?

3. Is there someone in your class you need to talk to about one of these issues? What do you think you need to say to that person?

4. What could you do today to begin making a difference in your school? What's keeping you from doing it?

5. Why do you think so many people judge others and label them so easily? What's really behind someone who consistently puts others down or labels them?

Family Reunion

Chapter 13

Guided Meditation

You feel a sense of excitement as your parents pull the car into the parking lot where this year's family reunion is being held. You have a ton of memories from previous reunions, but this one seems extra special to you for some reason.

As your family gets out of the car and begins unpacking all the stuff you brought along, you catch a glimpse of a few of your favorite people in the entire world; they must have arrived before you, and they're already busy playing together in the field next to the pavilion. Something inside you can't wait to run over and join them! What is it that makes these people so much fun? Why do you look forward to this every year?

Your parents ask you to help them get everything set up, and then you're off—running over to the field where everyone's playing. Who do you see first? What are you feeling as you run toward the rest of the family?

You can't believe you've got an entire day to simply enjoy being with the people you love the most. What do you hope to do? Who do you hope to see? If you could sit down and have a conversation with any member of your family, who would it be? Why? What would you hope to talk about?

As you think back to previous reunions, can you think of anyone missing this year? Why? Have members of your family passed away since your last reunion? How does that make you feel? What is your family missing as a result of their absence?

Your family is unique. There is no other family like yours in the entire world. Each member of your family makes a special contribution to this world. Who are you most thankful for? Why? Is there someone in your family who's difficult to be around? Why? What could you do to change that?

As the sun begins to set, you almost can't believe how fast the day has gone. What memories will you keep with you about this year's reunion? What do you look forward to next year?

Journal Entry

_____

_____

_____

_____

_____

_____

_____

_____

_____

Scripture Guides Us

Jesus' definition of his "family" has caused quite a few people to take a step back and think about the most important parts of their own families.

Take a few minutes to "chew on" the following Scripture verses, allowing God's Spirit to speak to you.

LUKE 14:26
"If anyone comes to me and does not hate father and mother, wife and children, brothers and sisters—yes, even life itself—such a person cannot be my disciple."

MARK 3:31-35
Then Jesus' mother and brothers arrived. Standing outside, they sent someone in to call him. A crowd was sitting around him, and they told him, "Your mother and brothers are outside looking for you." "Who are my mother and my brothers?" he asked. Then he looked at those seated in a circle around him and said, "Here are my mother and my brothers! Whoever does God's will is my brother and sister and mother."

Questions for Reflection

1. As you think about each of the members of your family, who do you wish you could get to know better? Why?

2. What is the greatest family memory you have?

3. What do you think Jesus means when he says you need to "hate" your father and mother, wife and children, brothers and sisters— yes, even your own life—or you cannot be his disciple?

4. Why do you think God put you in your family?

5. What unique contributions do you bring to your family?

6. Is there something about you that some other members of your family wish they could change? What do you think you should do about it?

7. What's the best part of your family? Why?

8. What would Jesus say to your family if he were at your reunion? Why?

Thanksgiving Day

Chapter 14

Guided Meditation

There are only a few mornings that you get to wake up and smell the aroma of turkey wafting through the air as you make your way into the kitchen, but today is a special day. Today is Thanksgiving! And what makes this Thanksgiving even more special is that everyone is coming to your house for the celebration.

As you walk into the living room, your parents ask you to help get the house ready for the big celebration. Your dad is busy setting up everything needed for the get-together. Your mom asks you to use the "special" dishes to set the table. You're eager to help because you're looking forward to seeing everyone again. As you set the table, you try to imagine where everyone will sit and what they'll talk about.

The day goes by quickly, and you barely have enough time to get everything ready before people begin arriving early in the afternoon. Everyone seems to have brought something to eat or drink. You wonder what you're going to do with all of this food. As the house begins filling up, what are you feeling inside? Who are you surprised to see? Is there anyone in your house who you'd rather not see? If you're more drawn to some people than to others, who are they? Why do you feel that way about them?

Your dad and mom are busy in the kitchen preparing the feast. As you glance that way, you see your dad carving up the bird, and several of your family members are standing around him, laughing. You wonder what's going on, but at that exact moment your dad calls everyone into the kitchen. It's almost time to eat. What happens next? Does your family have any Thanksgiving traditions that everyone participates in? Who takes the lead at this point? Does it seem as though some people are quieter? Why do you think that is?

As you eat a little bit of everything laid out before you, you remind yourself of how blessed you are compared to many people in our world. What's an appropriate response for your sense of gratefulness? Do you think other people at the table are feeling the same way?

As your family finishes dinner, everyone knows what's coming next...

Journal Entry

_____

_____

_____

_____

_____

_____

_____

_____

_____

Scripture Guides Us

It seems as though it's extremely difficult for many people to rise to gratefulness in our culture. Many people struggle with the idea of

giving thanks in all circumstances. Is thankfulness a difficult thing for you to practice in your everyday life? Or does it come easily to you?

Take a few minutes to "chew on" the following Scripture verses, allowing God's Spirit to speak to you.

HEBREWS 12:28
Therefore, since we are receiving a kingdom that cannot be shaken, let us be thankful, and so worship God acceptably with reverence and awe.

PSALM 100:4-5
Enter his gates with thanksgiving and his courts with praise; give thanks to him and praise his name. For the LORD is good and his love endures forever; his faithfulness continues through all generations.

PSALM 106:1
Give thanks to the LORD, for he is good; his love endures forever.

Questions for Reflection
1. What are some family traditions that mean a lot to you? Why do you think they are so important to you?

2. How important is thankfulness in your family? What could you do to become a more grateful person?

3. When do you find it most difficult to express thankfulness in your life? Why?

4. What are some possible alternatives you may have for dealing with all of the leftover food you end up with at Thanksgiving dinner? Is there a way you may be able to use it to serve someone with the love of Christ?

5. Why is it important to express your gratefulness in life? What might be the consequences of an ungrateful life?

6. What typically happens after Thanksgiving dinner at your house? What do you enjoy about that? What would you like to change?

7. What are some of the things you are most thankful for when it comes to your family? What are some of the things you wish you could change? What could you do about that?

8. What are some of the things you are most thankful for about your relationship with God? What are some of the things you wish you could change? What could you do about that?

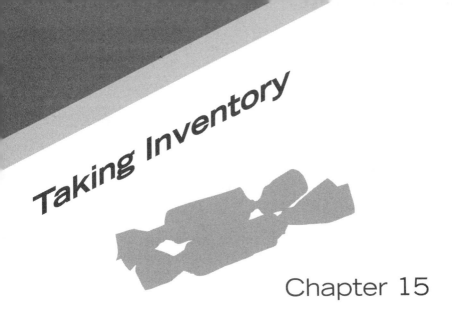

Chapter 15

Guided Meditation

Step outside your body for a while. Seriously, if you're able to do it, use your imagination to step away from yourself for a few minutes. Let's spend some time watching you today. Let's watch as you go about a normal day in your life to see what we can learn.

It's amazing what we can see when we step back and look at something in a fresh, new way, isn't it? Sometimes we see things we like, and other times we may see some things that need to change.

So, what do you notice about yourself? What do you notice about the way you treat people? How you speak to them? How you respond to their questions?

Let's start with the people who know you best: Your own family. Have you ever heard the old saying, "Familiarity breeds contempt"? What it means is that we can become so close to certain people that we sometimes don't realize how badly we treat them. Could this be said about you and the way you treat your family members? Why do you think you respond to certain things that happen around your house the way you do?

Imagine yourself standing outside your body holding a clipboard and a pencil. You're taking an inventory of your life. What are some of the things you like about yourself and the way you treat people? If you're finding a lot of negatives, what would it take to turn over a new leaf and start over again? What's holding you back? Is it your reputation? What people would think about you?

What about with your friends at school? What would they say about you and the way you interact with them? Would they characterize you as a kind person? Someone who cares about them and is patient with them through difficult times? What about your teachers?

As you look at yourself going about your day, what do you like about the way you interact with those in authority over you? What needs to change?

Not many people have the opportunity to make the kind of positive changes that are available to you. Many people think it's too late. What do you think? And more importantly, what will you do about it? An inventory is only as good as the action it produces.

Journal Entry

_____

_____

_____

_____

_____

_____

_____

_____

_____

_____

Scripture Guides Us

How do you measure your spirituality? Are you a better Christ-follower because you often read your Bible or pray? Or should you measure your spirituality by the thoughts, attitudes, and actions that flow out of your life?

Take a few minutes to "chew on" the following Scripture verses, allowing God's Spirit to speak to you.

GALATIANS 5:22-23

But the fruit of the Spirit is love, joy, peace, patience, kindness, goodness, faithfulness, gentleness and self-control.

Questions for Reflection

1. What do you think Galatians 5:22-23 means when it refers to the fruit of the Spirit?

2. How loving are you?

3. Who do you have a difficult time loving? Why? What could you do about it?

4. What are the things that bring the most joy into your life? What saps the joy out of you?

83

5. Describe yourself when you are completely at peace.

6. What makes it most difficult for you to practice patience?

7. What's your plan for becoming a person characterized by kindness?

8. What are some good things you've done lately? How did they make you feel?

9. What does it mean for you to be faithful?

10. How could you become a gentler person?

11. When do you find it most difficult to exercise self-control in your life? What could you do to develop a stronger degree of self-control?

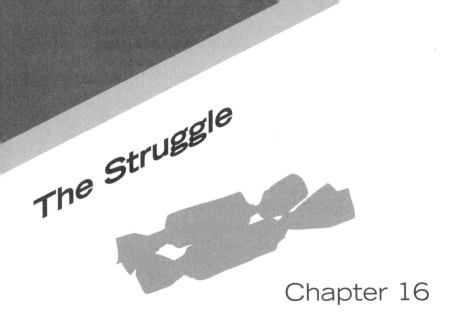

The Struggle

Chapter 16

Guided Meditation

It seems you've been here so many times before. You've battled this same temptation for years and wish you could finally put it behind you. Your heart is pounding through your chest. You can literally feel your body reacting to it. Your hands are shaking. You don't want to go down this road again, but something inside of you wants to do it. So many voices in your head right now are all saying different things. What are you going to do? How did you get here again, anyway? Maybe it's because you hurt so bad inside. The pain is too much to bear. Why do you always seem to end up struggling with this same issue?

As you lean back to take a deep breath and try to think this whole thing through, you start noting some of the consequences of your actions. What happens when you give in to this particular temptation? Who else are you affecting beside yourself? Does anyone else have to know? Should you keep your struggle a secret? How's that working out for you? Is the secrecy making it better or worse?

Then you hear a voice in your head saying, "Maybe it's time to do things differently. Maybe it's time to finally come out with this and make a change."

As you listen to yourself talking it through in your head, you realize your heart is still pounding; your body is still reacting. There's a huge part of you that simply wants to give in to this and get it over with. It seems inevitable. After everything you've been through, don't you deserve this? You're hungry, you're lonely, you're angry, and you're tired of it all. Maybe it's easier to give in just this one time. After all, can't you just confess it to God, ask for forgiveness, and get a fresh start anyway? What could it hurt?

But then you hear another voice in your head telling you to fight it. You remember hearing someone tell you that you start to discover what kind of person you are when no one's watching. You find out who you are when you're alone, facing difficult decisions.

So what are you going to do? What kind of person are you?

Journal Entry

_____

_____

_____

_____

_____

_____

_____

_____

_____

_____

Scripture Guides Us

Someone once said, "Character is who you are when no one's looking." So based on that definition, what kind of person are you? What are

you doing to train and prepare yourself for the temptations that will inevitably come into your life?

Take a few minutes to "chew on" the following Scripture verses, allowing God's Spirit to speak to you.

1 CORINTHIANS 10:13

No temptation has overtaken you except what is common to us all. And God is faithful; he will not let you be tempted beyond what you can bear. But when you are tempted, he will also provide a way out so that you can endure it.

ROMANS 7:18-21

I know that good itself does not dwell in me, that is, in my sinful nature. For I have the desire to do what is good, but I cannot carry it out. For I do not do the good I want to do; but the evil I do not want to do—this I keep on doing. Now if I do what I do not want to do, it is no longer I who do it, but it is sin living in me that does it. So I find this law at work: Although I want to do good, evil is right there with me.

MATTHEW 6:13

"And lead us not into temptation, but deliver us from the evil one."

Questions for Reflection

1. What's one of the biggest temptations you're facing right now?

2. Have you ever experienced God providing a way out for you during your temptation? Describe that experience.

3. How do you think shame affects us when we're in the middle of struggling with temptation?

4. Have you ever felt your body physically react to a particular temptation you faced? How did you handle it?

5. What are some of the triggers that make you more susceptible to temptation? Are you more prone to struggle with temptation when you're hungry, angry, lonely, or tired?

6. What role does secrecy play in your battle with temptation?

7. What would it look like for you to let someone else into your struggle? How could that possibly help you?

8. Do you think you're keeping your struggle a secret from God? How would it change your approach to battling temptation if you understood that God already knew about it? What if you really believed that God's right there with you in the temptation, and no matter what, God loves you?

9. What role does prayer play in your struggle with temptation?

In the Still of the Night

Chapter 17

Guided Meditation

You're going through your normal routine getting ready to go to bed. It's been a very long day, and you have a lot on your mind. So much has happened in the last several hours, it almost seems like it's been two or three days rolled into one. Is it difficult for you to shut off your mind and fall asleep? What are you thinking about?

As you jump into bed and pull the covers under your chin, you take a deep breath and stare up at the ceiling. Your mind is still racing. A million things are flying through your brain, so you take a few deep breaths and try to calm down. Then a few minutes later you finally hear it. You lie there quietly for a little longer to make sure that's what it is, because it's been so long since you've heard it. As you lie in the dark listening, what you hear is the deep silence of the night thundering back at you. As your breathing eventually slows, you can hear your heart beating in your ears, it's so quiet. No doors are creaking. No wind is blowing outside. Just peace and quiet. It's been a while since you've experienced this kind of silence, and to be completely honest, you're intrigued by it. You wonder why you can't find this kind of quiet in your life on a regular basis.

What are you thinking about as you lie there in the dark? What's going through your mind? As you lie there for a few more minutes, about ready to drift off to sleep, you hear a quiet whisper in the distance. It's muffled at first and pretty tough to hear, so you find yourself sitting straight up in bed, trying to hear better. Silence echoes back. You could've sworn you heard something, but after a few more minutes of waiting, you lie back down and try to fall asleep. Then suddenly you hear it again. This time it's much louder than a whisper and much more distinct.

You rip off the covers and walk into the hallway near your bedroom, almost expecting to see someone out there, but there's no one. You're confused, and now you're getting frustrated. Is someone playing a joke on you? C'mon. It's been a long day already. Why can't they just leave you alone so you can get some sleep?

As you head back to your room and sit down on the edge of your bed, something happens that you'll never forget. Standing on the other side of your room is an angel who's smiling and looking right at you. The angel seems to have a message for you. This is what you heard before in the darkness! Your eyes are as big as saucers as you wait to hear what the angel has to say to you. You've never experienced anything like this before.

Journal Entry

_____

_____

_____

_____

_____

_____

_____

_____

_____

_____

Scripture Guides Us

The God of the Bible is a God of communication. God is communicating with us all the time in many different ways. Unfortunately we seldom take the time to listen for God's voice. What are some of the ways you have experienced God speaking to you personally? What helps you hear God more clearly?

Take a few minutes to "chew on" the following Scripture verses, allowing God's Spirit to speak to you.

PSALM 46:10-11

"Be still, and know that I am God; I will be exalted among the nations, I will be exalted in the earth." The LORD Almighty is with us; the God of Jacob is our fortress.

1 SAMUEL 3:2-11

One night Eli, whose eyes were becoming so weak that he could barely see, was lying down in his usual place. The lamp of God had not yet gone out, and Samuel was lying down in the house of the LORD, where the ark of God was. Then the LORD called Samuel. Samuel answered, "Here I am." And he ran to Eli and said, "Here I am; you called me." But Eli said, "I did not call; go back and lie down." So he went and lay down. Again the LORD called, "Samuel!" And Samuel got up and went to Eli and said, "Here I am; you called me." "My son," Eli said, "I did not call; go back and lie down." Now Samuel did not yet know the LORD: The word of the LORD had not yet been revealed to him. A third time the LORD called, "Samuel." And Samuel got up and went to Eli and said, "Here I am; you called me." Then Eli realized that the LORD was calling the boy. So Eli told Samuel, "Go and lie down, and if he calls you, say, 'Speak, LORD, for your servant is listening.'" So Samuel went and lay down in his place. The LORD came and stood there, calling as at the other times, "Samuel! Samuel!" Then Samuel said, "Speak, for your servant is listening." And the LORD said to Samuel: "See, I am about to do something in Israel that will make the ears of everyone who hears about it tingle."

Questions for Reflection

1. How do you clear your mind when it won't allow you to relax?

2. It seems as though many people have a hard time experiencing silence. Why do you think that is? Where could you find a few silent pockets in your day?

3. Why do you think it's so difficult for most people to hear God speak today?

4. Where and when do you find it easiest to hear God's voice?

5. What do you think the Bible means when it says, "Be still, and know that I am God"?

6. Have you ever heard about people who've had an experience like the one we just read about where God or an angel communicates directly to them? What do you think about these kinds of things?

7. Eli tells Samuel to pray a simple prayer: "Speak Lord, for your servant is listening." How could that prayer help you today?

Hide and Seek

Chapter 18

Guided Meditation

"One, two, three, four..." You hear your friend start counting to 30 while you and everyone else run away to find places to hide. It's been a long time since you've played this silly game, but it sure brings back a lot of great memories. You always had so much fun playing Hide and Seek when you were younger. You can hardly believe you and all your friends are enjoying the game even though you're so much older.

As you run down the hallway, you think of a million different potential hiding places, but you decide to go for that special spot that you're sure no one else knows about. You crawl into your secret space. You cover up with a blanket so no one will see you. You're still breathing hard from running so fast, and you're sure everyone can hear your heart beating through your chest.

By the time you settle back into your hiding place, you can hear your friend finish counting, "28, 29, 30. Ready or not, here I come!"

As your friend starts running down hallways and opening doors, you can hear others quickly being discovered. Lots of laughter and yelling come through the walls from the other rooms, but you remain hidden away where no one can find you.

At that moment you hear some voices getting closer to where you're hiding. They're whispering something. You can barely make out what they're saying. What is it? Are they talking about you? Do they know where you are? Or worse yet, do they see you? As you peek out from under the corner of the blanket you've draped over the top of your body, you see your friends' feet inches away from your hiding place. You hold your breath, hoping they won't see you. After a few seconds they turn and walk away. You exhale slowly while a sly smile comes across your face. You did it! You fooled them. They were right next to you, but didn't notice you. How does that make you feel?

Several more minutes go by, and now you can hear everyone else yelling your name; they're begging you to come out from wherever you're hiding. They've looked everywhere and couldn't find you. So what are you going to do? Is it time for you to come out of hiding? Are you going to tell them where you were or continue to keep it a secret?

Journal Entry

Scripture Guides Us

In the following story Jesus tells us about the lost sheep, about the importance God places upon us as individuals. He notices when one little one is missing, and there's absolutely nowhere we can hide where

he isn't. Jesus is already there waiting to take us into his arms and show us how much he loves us.

Take a few minutes to "chew on" the following Scripture verses, allowing God's Spirit to speak to you.

LUKE 15:4-7

"Suppose one of you has a hundred sheep and loses one of them. Doesn't he leave the ninety-nine in the open country and go after the lost sheep until he finds it? And when he finds it, he joyfully puts it on his shoulders and goes home. Then he calls his friends and neighbors together and says, 'Rejoice with me; I have found my lost sheep.' I tell you that in the same way there will be more rejoicing in heaven over one sinner who repents than over ninety-nine righteous persons who do not need to repent."

Questions for Reflection

1. Have you ever wanted to hide where no one could find you? What makes you feel that way at times?

2. Are there certain places where you feel safer than others? What makes you feel that way?

3. What things in your life make you want to go into hiding?

4. Are there any parts of your life that you're trying to keep hidden from people? What makes you want to keep these things hidden?

5. How does it make you feel to know that there's absolutely nowhere you can go to hide from God? How is it possible for God to be everywhere all at the same time?

6. Why do you think the one lost sheep is so important to the person who loses it in Luke 15?

Steer Clear

Chapter 19

Guided Meditation

You've been waiting for this day for a long time. You can remember those days when you were much younger, and you pretended to be a race-car driver. You weren't even big enough to see above the dashboard, but you couldn't wait to experience what it felt like to get behind the wheel of a car. And today you're actually going for your driver's license.

You've studied hard and even passed the written test, but now this is where the rubber meets the road. Literally. For weeks your friends have been asking if you're nervous about taking the driving test. What have you been telling them? How are you feeling about all of this as you pull into the Department of Motor Vehicles parking lot? Are you ready?

As you stand in line waiting for your name to be called, you watch some student drivers coming back from their tests. Some have smiles on their faces and seem completely relieved. Others, however, look pretty disappointed in themselves. You can tell that the test must not be as easy as everyone told you—at least for some people. How do you think you'll feel when you're finished with your test?

While you continue waiting in line, you find yourself deep in thought until you're suddenly jolted back to reality when you hear your name called. You can't believe it, but it's your turn. The instructor comes from behind the desk to greet you, gets your paperwork, and then asks you to pull your car up in front to get ready to go.

While you're pulling the car up, you notice your instructor walking toward you. A million things are running through your mind right now and you're trying to remember them all. Wear your seatbelt. Turn off the radio. Don't forget to use your turn signal. You tell yourself to try and calm down. Take a deep breath. Relax. Everything's going to work out fine. So then...why are your hands shaking as you grip the steering wheel?

The instructor is walking over to your car. You're almost ready to go. As she's opening the door, you decide to offer up a silent prayer. What do you say to God? What do you want God to do?

Journal Entry

_____

_____

_____

_____

_____

_____

_____

_____

_____

Scripture Guides Us

Many people struggle with worry and anxiety. It seems difficult for them to let go of control over their lives and turn it over to God. Why do you think that's so tough for some people? Is God difficult to trust with

our worries and fears? Or is God capable of handling the issues we face in our lives?

Take a few minutes to "chew on" the following Scripture verses, allowing God's Spirit to speak to you.

MATTHEW 6:25-34

"Therefore I tell you, do not worry about your life, what you will eat or drink; or about your body, what you will wear. Is not life more important than food, and the body more important than clothes? Look at the birds of the air; they do not sow or reap or store away in barns, and yet your heavenly Father feeds them. Are you not much more valuable than they? Can any of you by worrying add a single hour to your life? And why do you worry about clothes? See how the lilies of the field grow. They do not labor or spin. Yet I tell you that not even Solomon in all his splendor was dressed like one of these. If that is how God clothes the grass of the field, which is here today and tomorrow is thrown into the fire, will he not much more clothe you—you of little faith? So do not worry, saying, 'What shall we eat?' or 'What shall we drink?' or 'What shall we wear?' For the pagans run after all these things, and your heavenly Father knows that you need them. But seek first his kingdom and his righteousness, and all these things will be given to you as well. Therefore do not worry about tomorrow, for tomorrow will worry about itself. Each day has enough trouble of its own."

1 PETER 5:7

Cast all your anxiety on him because he cares for you.

PSALM 94:18-19

When I said, "My foot is slipping," your unfailing love, LORD, supported me. When anxiety was great within me, your consolation brought me joy.

Questions for Reflection

1. What are some of the things in your life that make you feel nervous or anxious? How do you respond to them?

2. What are some of the biggest tests you've faced in your life? How have you responded to these tests? What would you do differently in the future?

3. How can prayer help in stressful times?

4. How do our failures have the potential to make us stronger?

5. In Matthew 6 Jesus encourages us to seek first the Kingdom of God. How can this help us in our struggle with anxiety?

6. What do you think it means to cast all your anxiety on God? Why should we consider doing this, according to 1 Peter 5:7?

7. According to the psalmist, when worry and stress build inside us, we can find joy in our relationships with God. How does your relationship with Jesus bring you joy in challenging times?

Who Are You, Really?

Chapter 20

Guided Meditation

You're enjoying another beautiful warm day as you lay outside on your hammock, staring at the puffy clouds. You're alone, and you're deep in thought. You're wondering about who you really are—at the core. You know...what's your true identity? What do you really like to do? What do the people you know best say about you? What kind of person would they say you are?

You don't often find yourself this deep in thought on a sunny afternoon, but a lot of stuff has been happening in your life lately. Certain things have caused you to ask these questions.

You focus for a while on what you're good at. What are some of the first things that come to mind? Some of your friends are good at sports and you've noticed that almost everyone labels them that way—as jocks. So how do the things you enjoy doing define you? What are you into and how does it contribute to your identity?

Then you find yourself thinking about another aspect of your life. A few days earlier, your teacher asked your class a question: If your house were on fire, and you were running out to save yourself and had a split second to grab a couple of your most important possessions, what would they be and why? Ever since, you can't seem to get this question out of your mind. As you've thought about this, you've wondered how your possessions define who you are.

So who are you really? Can you be identified by what you do? Can you be identified by what other people say or don't say about you? Or are you identified by all of the stuff you own? Who are you deep down inside? And why is it important, anyway?

Journal Entry

_____

_____

_____

_____

_____

_____

_____

_____

_____

Scripture Guides Us

When Jesus is tempted by the devil in the desert, the devil appeals to three basic areas of Jesus' identity in the temptation. Will Jesus define himself by what he can do? By what he can have? By what other people will say about him? Or will Jesus find his identity in something else?

Take a few minutes to "chew on" the following Scripture verses, allowing God's Spirit to speak to you.

MATTHEW 4:1-11

Then Jesus was led by the Spirit into the wilderness to be tempted by the devil. After fasting forty days and forty nights, he was hungry. The

tempter came to him and said, "If you are the Son of God, tell these stones to become bread." Jesus answered, "It is written: 'People do not live on bread alone, but on every word that comes from the mouth of God.'" Then the devil took him to the holy city and had him stand on the highest point of the temple. "If you are the Son of God," he said, "throw yourself down. For it is written: 'He will command his angels concerning you, and they will lift you up in their hands, so that you will not strike your foot against a stone.'" Jesus answered him, "It is also written: 'Do not put the Lord your God to the test.'" Again, the devil took him to a very high mountain and showed him all the kingdoms of the world and their splendor. "All this I will give you," he said, "if you will bow down and worship me." Jesus said to him, "Away from me, Satan! For it is written: 'Worship the Lord your God, and serve him only.'" Then the devil left him, and angels came and attended him.

COLOSSIANS 2:9-10
For in Christ all the fullness of the Deity lives in bodily form, and in Christ you have been brought to fullness. He is the head over every power and authority.

MATTHEW 3:13-17
Then Jesus came from Galilee to the Jordan to be baptized by John. But John tried to deter him, saying, "I need to be baptized by you, and do you come to me?" Jesus replied, "Let it be so now; it is proper for us to do this to fulfill all righteousness." Then John consented. As soon as Jesus was baptized, he went up out of the water. At that moment heaven was opened, and he saw the Spirit of God descending like a dove and alighting on him. And a voice from heaven said, "This is my Son, whom I love; with him I am well pleased."

Questions for Reflection

1. When you have deep thoughts about your life and who you are at your core, what are some of the things you come up with?

2. How would your closest friends identify you? What would they say you value most? Why?

3. Why is it so important for us to know who we are, anyway?

4. Think about what most guys talk about soon after meeting for the first time. Don't they usually want to know, "So what do you do for a living?" Why do you think that's so important to most guys? How can what they do for a living become a major part of their identities?

5. Now think about how most girls identify themselves. How is it different from the way the guys identify themselves? Why do you think that is?

6. When the devil tempts Jesus to turn the stone to bread in Matthew 4, he's tempting Jesus to find his identity in what he can DO. How does Jesus respond to this temptation?

7. Notice how the devil also quotes Scripture before he tempts Jesus with the opportunity to define himself by what he could HAVE (all the kingdoms of the world). How does Jesus respond to Satan's temptation this time?

8. Finally, the devil asks Jesus to throw himself off the top of the temple and be rescued by the angels because he knows how all the people worshiping in the temple at the time would react and what they would SAY about Jesus. How does Jesus respond to the devil's temptation to define himself by what people might say about him? How do you handle this same temptation to define yourself by what others might say or not say about you?

9. According to Colossians 2:9-10, what should we rely on as the true basis of our identities?

10. At Jesus' baptism in Matthew 3, God the Father has a couple of very important things to say about his Son in verse 17. What are those things, and why do you think they're such important parts of anyone's true identity?

The First Snow

Chapter 21

Guided Meditation

It's finally here! The first snow of the season. As you look out the window of your home, you see thousands of huge snowflakes falling from the sky. You feel completely blown away by the beauty of the scene...so white and pure. It's already late in the day, but it's snowing so hard, you're wondering what it will look like in the morning if it continues snowing all night. Later, as you jump into bed and begin drifting off to sleep, what are you thinking of? What do you think you'll be dreaming about tonight?

In the morning, you bolt out of bed and rush over to the window. It's just as you suspected; nothing but white for as far as you can see. Then your mom comes into your room to tell you that school is canceled for the day—your dream has come true! She tells you to go back to bed, but you can hardly wait to get your snow gear on and go outside to enjoy the snow. There's no way you're ever going to be able to fall back to sleep at this point anyway, so you grab a quick breakfast and start getting ready.

After you get all your winter gear on, you head out into the snow. What does it feel like under your feet? What does it look like? The first thing you want to do is walk toward the middle of your yard and fall backward into the snow and make a snow angel. As you're lying there with your arms and legs scraping the snow like long plows, you notice the intricacy of each of the tiny snowflakes landing on your body. Each one is unique, so incredibly detailed. Why do you think God would add that much detail to something as simple as a snowflake?

As you sit up and take a look around, the one thing that hits you is how quiet your neighborhood is this morning. The snow acts almost like a natural insulator and makes everything so peaceful. Then you see some of your friends making their way outside to join you. You can't wait to experience this first snow with them. What will you and your friends do together on this special day?

Journal Entry

_____

_____

_____

_____

_____

_____

_____

_____

_____

Scripture Guides Us

In the verses from the book of Job, God is responding to Job's questions about who's in charge of the earth and everything that happens here. Job has come across as if he thinks he's smarter than God, so God has a few random questions for Job.

Psalm 51 was written by King David after his sin of adultery with Bathsheba and the murder of her husband, Uriah. In the Psalm, David records his confession and begs for God's forgiveness.

Take a few minutes to "chew on" the following Scripture verses, allowing God's Spirit to speak to you.

JOB 38:18-23

"Have you comprehended the vast expanses of the earth? Tell me, if you know all this. What is the way to the abode of light? And where does darkness reside? Can you take them to their places? Do you know the paths to their dwellings? Surely you know, for you were already born! You have lived so many years! Have you entered the storehouses of the snow or seen the storehouses of the hail, which I reserve for times of trouble, for days of war and battle?"

ISAIAH 1:18

"Come now, let us reason together," says the LORD. "Though your sins are like scarlet, they shall be as white as snow; though they are red as crimson, they shall be like wool."

PSALM 51:1-10

Have mercy on me, O God, according to your unfailing love; according to your great compassion blot out my transgressions. Wash away all my iniquity and cleanse me from my sin. For I know my transgressions, and my sin is always before me. Against you, you only, have I sinned and done what is evil in your sight, so that you are right in your verdict and justified when you judge. Surely I was sinful at birth, sinful from the time my mother conceived me. Yet you desired faithfulness even in the womb; you taught me wisdom in that secret place. Cleanse me with hyssop, and I will be clean; wash me, and I will be whiter than snow. Let me hear joy and gladness; let the bones you have crushed rejoice. Hide your face from my sins and blot out all my iniquity. Create in me a pure heart, O God, and renew a steadfast spirit within me.

Questions for Reflection

1. In this meditation, you were very excited about the anticipated snowfall. What are you genuinely excited about in your life right now? Is there something you're anticipating in the near future that you can't wait to experience?

2. Have you ever experienced the first snowfall of the season? How does it make you feel? What are some of the things you enjoy most about the snow?

3. What does the intricate design of a simple snowflake tell you about the nature and character of God? How much value do you think God places upon beauty? Why do you think that is? How does that beauty point us to God?

4. Why does snow remind us of purity? What are some areas of your life you'd like to experience a greater degree of purity in right now? What can you do about it?

5. How does God's response to Job in Job 38 make you feel about God's involvement in our universe? Why is that so important?

6. Have you ever asked God to wash away your sin and make you "white as snow"? How does it make you feel to experience God's cleansing power that's available to you through his Son Jesus?

7. What does David's experience of God's forgiveness in Psalm 51 tell us about our own process of confession and forgiveness? How is it possible for us to receive the forgiveness of God?

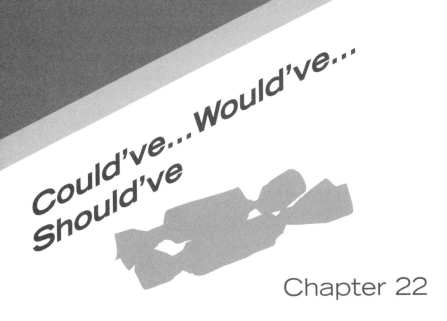

Could've...Would've...
Should've

Chapter 22

Guided Meditation

You have so many thoughts and feelings rushing through your mind all at once. On one hand, you can't wait to experience what's ahead of you today. What are you about to do? It's a once-in-a-lifetime opportunity, isn't it? You've been looking forward to this your entire life, and you can't believe you've been given this opportunity—it's almost surreal. On the other hand, you're scared to death because you've never attempted anything like this before.

The minutes click by and you're closer and closer to actually going through with it. You sense a huge knot growing in your stomach. The fear is beginning to overwhelm you. Maybe you should back out. There's sure to be another opportunity somewhere down the road, right?

But then you consider what all of your friends will think if you back out. Many of them have encouraged you to give this a shot, and you know you'll be disappointed if you choose not to go through with it. But who's making this decision, anyway? You are so conflicted you begin to feel sick. What decision are you going to make?

Finally the moment of truth arrives. Your heart is racing. Your hands are shaking. It feels like everyone is looking at you, waiting to see what you're going to do. So what will it be? Are you going to step up and do it? Or are you going to back away and wait for another opportunity?

Journal Entry

_____

_____

_____

_____

_____

_____

_____

_____

_____

Scripture Guides Us

It seems as though fear keeps a lot of people from doing the things they genuinely want to do. What role does fear play in your life? Has there ever been a time when you backed out of something that you wanted to do and then you haven't yet received another chance to do it? What does the Bible say about fear and how it should affect our lives?

Take a few minutes to "chew on" the following Scripture verses, allowing God's Spirit to speak to you.

1 JOHN 4:18

There is no fear in love. But perfect love drives out fear, because fear has to do with punishment. The one who fears is not made perfect in love.

LUKE 12:4-5

"I tell you, my friends, do not be afraid of those who kill the body and after that can do no more. But I will show you whom you should fear:

Fear him who, after your body has been killed, has authority to throw you into hell. Yes, I tell you, fear him."

PSALM 23:4
Even though I walk through the darkest valley, I will fear no evil, for you are with me; your rod and your staff, they comfort me.

Questions for Reflection

1. Think of a time in your life when you were afraid to do something, but you went ahead and did it anyway. What happened? How did you feel afterward?

2. Think of a time in your life when fear kept you from doing something. What happened? How did you feel afterward?

3. Have you ever had to live with the regret of not doing something you wished you had done? How did that make you feel? What would you do differently if you had it to do all over again?

4. Name the things you're most afraid of. Why do you think you're so afraid of these things? What may help you work through your fears?

5. What do you think the Bible means when it says, "Perfect love drives out fear"? What is perfect love? Why do you think it has this effect on fear?

6. What did Jesus have to say about fear in Luke 12:4-5? How do these verses make you feel?

7. David seems to be walking through some incredibly fear-filled times in Psalm 23. What does he do to help manage his fear? How could this same technique help you?

Oh, to Be Young Again

Chapter 23

Guided Meditation

Blowing bubbles. Jumping on a trampoline. Running through the sprinkler. Playing catch. Popping bubble wrap. Dancing. Singing. Jumping in puddles. Use your imagination to remember a time when you were a little kid, and you were simply playing around and enjoying yourself. What do you imagine yourself doing? Who would you be playing with? What makes it so much fun?

Certain things in life are meant to be enjoyed. There are certain activities that God created to bring us joy. What are those things in your life? In a world where seriousness and responsibility can easily steal our joy and happiness, it's important to stay connected to the "little kid" inside of you that simply wants to play and live life carefree and innocent.

As you imagine yourself enjoying whatever it is you're doing, what are the people who know you best saying to you? Are they encouraging you to keep playing? Or are they telling you to grow up and stop goofing around? And is growing up everything you thought it would be? Why does it seem like so often growing up means getting dull and boring? Why do some people seem to understand the importance of delighting in play, while others seem to discourage you from childlike fun?

Journal Entry

_____

_____

_____

_____

_____

_____

_____

_____

_____

_____

Scripture Guides Us

Jesus spent quite a bit of time talking about the importance of becoming like a little child if we want to experience the Kingdom of God. What do you think he meant by that?

Take a few minutes to "chew on" the following Scripture verses, allowing God's Spirit to speak to you.

LUKE 18:15-17

People were also bringing babies to Jesus to have him place his hands on them. When the disciples saw this, they rebuked them. But Jesus called the children to him and said, "Let the little children come to me, and do not hinder them, for the kingdom of God belongs to such as these. Truly I tell you, anyone who will not receive the kingdom of God like a little child will never enter it."

MATTHEW 18:2-6

He called a little child, whom he placed among them. And he said: "Truly I tell you, unless you change and become like little children,

you will never enter the kingdom of heaven. Therefore, whoever takes a humble place—becoming like this child—is the greatest in the kingdom of heaven. And whoever welcomes one such little child in my name welcomes me. If anyone causes one of these little ones—those who believe in me—to stumble, it would be better for them if a large millstone was hung around their neck and they were drowned in the depths of the sea."

HEBREWS 12:2
...Fixing our eyes on Jesus, the pioneer and perfecter of faith. For the joy set before him he endured the cross, scorning its shame, and sat down at the right hand of the throne of God.

ROMANS 15:13
May the God of hope fill you with all joy and peace as you trust in him, so that you may overflow with hope by the power of the Holy Spirit.

Questions for Reflection
1. What did "playing" look like when you were a little kid?

2. Who did you enjoy playing with when you were a little kid? Why?

3. What are you doing to make sure you never lose your childlike playfulness? Why is it so important not to lose touch with this part of you?

4. How does it make you feel to know that God enjoys watching you "play"?

5. What do you think Jesus means when he says the Kingdom of heaven belongs to the little children?

6. What point do you think Jesus is trying to make in Matthew 18:2-6 when he has the little child stand among those he's teaching?

7. What kind of joy do you think Jesus experienced on his way to the cross?

8. What brings you the most joy in your life today? How do you handle those days when it's extremely hard to find any joy?

First Date

Chapter 24

Guided Meditation

You've been looking forward to this for a long time. Tonight will be your first official date! You've heard a lot about how this night is supposed to go and what you're supposed to do, and now you're actually going to live it out. What are you feeling as the time gets closer? Are you nervous? Excited? Maybe a little of both?

A lot of people have been giving you advice about your date. Who are the loudest voices? What are they saying? Are you surprised by any of the things they're telling you? What are your expectations for the evening? What are you looking forward to? What are you a little nervous about?

As you start getting ready for the big night, what are some of the most important things you need to do to prepare? Have you thought about what you're going to wear? Where are you planning to go? What are you going to do together? Do you think it will be easy to talk? Or do you think you'll have to work hard to have a conversation?

Hundreds of questions are racing through your mind as you're getting ready for your date. What attracted you to this person in the first place? What do you like about this person? What character qualities do you see that are attractive to you?

Chew on This

As you finish getting ready, your parents are calling you out of your room; they want to talk with you about your date. What advice do you think they'll give you? How do you feel about their interest in what you're doing tonight?

After a few minutes, you look at your watch and realize that it's almost time to go. Your parents stand up and give you a huge hug. They seem pretty emotional. What happens next? Imagine how your evening will go.

Journal Entry

_____

_____

_____

_____

_____

_____

_____

_____

_____

Scripture Guides Us

What are some biblical principles that we can apply to the dating experience? The Bible talks a lot about what true love is. It also talks about the importance of relying on God's wisdom to help us make good choices.

Take a few minutes to "chew on" the following Scripture verses, allowing God's Spirit to speak to you.

PSALM 90:12
Teach us to number our days, that we may gain a heart of wisdom.

PROVERBS 3:5-6
Trust in the LORD with all your heart and lean not on your own understanding; in all your ways submit to him, and he will make your paths straight.

PROVERBS 16:9
In their hearts human beings plan their course, but the LORD establishes their steps.

1 CORINTHIANS 13:4-8
Love is patient, love is kind. It does not envy, it does not boast, it is not proud. It does not dishonor others, it is not self-seeking, it is not easily angered, it keeps no record of wrongs. Love does not delight in evil but rejoices with the truth. It always protects, always trusts, always hopes, always perseveres. Love never fails.

Questions for Reflection

1. If you've already been on your first date, what was it like? What would you do differently if you could do it all over again? If you've not been on your first date yet, what are you looking forward to the most? What are you nervous about?

2. What do you think the best parts of the dating experience are? What are the worst parts?

3. What are some of your expectations about the dating relationship? How do you think your expectations line up with God's expectations?

4. What are some of the purposes for dating someone?

5. What are some of the dangers in any dating relationship? What could you do to avoid some of those dangers?

6. What kinds of pressures have you felt about going out on a date with someone?

7. Why do you think wisdom is such an important part of the dating relationship?

8. How can you tell when you love someone? According to 1 Corinthians 13, what is real love like? How can you incorporate that kind of love into all of your relationships?

Talk to Me

Chapter 25

Guided Meditation

It's a normal day like any other. You're busy doing what you do. But as you go about your daily routine, you sense someone wanting to spend time with you. He wants you to come to him. He wants you to be with him. You definitely recognize his voice, but it's been a while since you've spent any real time together. Doesn't he know how busy your life can be? After all, you've been busy doing what you do.

He sits there, hunkered down in the corner of your room waiting for you. He's certainly not pushing himself on you, but you can definitely tell he longs to spend some time with you. You tell him that you don't think you'll have time to meet with him today as you head out the door again.

When you get back from your day, he's there again, waiting for you. He smiles at you as you come in the door and asks you how your day has been. He invites you to sit down and rest for a while. You can tell he wants to hear about your day and everything else you've got going on in your life. He seems very proud of who you are becoming. He asks you about what seems to be pressing in on you and weighing you down. You can tell he genuinely cares about you. He wants what's best for you. So you finally decide to sit down for a few minutes to talk with him.

You start by telling him that you can't talk long because you still have a lot to do before bedtime. But after a few minutes of talking together, your whole world and all the worries of your day seem to simply melt away. You haven't felt this relaxed in a long time. You find yourself pouring your heart out to him. And then he looks you right in the eyes and tells you how proud he is of you. He tells you how much he loves you and enjoys spending time together.

At that moment you realize this friend who has been waiting to talk with you day after day is Jesus. He has never made you feel guilty about blowing him off day after day. He looks at you and smiles. It's at that moment that you can tell for the first time in your life that you have a true friend who cares about you for who you are. The time seems to fly by as you continue talking together late into the night.

Journal Entry

Scripture Guides Us

Would it surprise you to hear that Jesus enjoys spending time with you? He loves you like crazy and just enjoys being with you. But he'll never force himself upon you. He'll simply wait until you're ready to be with

him. And somehow it always ends up being some of the best time of your entire day.

Take a few minutes to "chew on" the following Scripture verses, allowing God's Spirit to speak to you.

MATTHEW 11:28-30

"Come to me, all you who are weary and burdened, and I will give you rest. Take my yoke upon you and learn from me, for I am gentle and humble in heart, and you will find rest for your souls. For my yoke is easy and my burden is light."

PSALM 16:7-10

I will praise the LORD, who counsels me; even at night my heart instructs me. I keep my eyes always on the LORD. With him at my right hand, I will not be shaken. Therefore my heart is glad and my tongue rejoices; my body also will rest secure, because you will not abandon me to the realm of the dead, nor will you let your faithful one see decay.

PSALM 32:6-7

Therefore let all the faithful pray to you while you may be found; surely the rising mighty waters will not reach them. You are my hiding place; you will protect me from trouble and surround me with songs of deliverance.

PSALM 62:1-2

Truly my soul finds rest in God; my salvation comes from him. Truly he is my rock and my salvation; he is my fortress, I will never be shaken.

1 THESSALONIANS 5:17

Pray continually.

Questions for Reflection

1. What does it look like for you to spend time with Jesus? What do you enjoy most about your time with him? What are some of the obstacles that prevent you from spending time with him?

2. Think about some of the best times you've had connecting with God. What made them so special? How could you make that happen more often?

3. How does busy-ness and your schedule keep you from spending time with God? What things could you stop doing in order to spend some more time with him?

4. What does Matthew 11:28-30 say about the yoke Jesus offers us? What does it make you feel like to know that Jesus is carrying that yoke along with you?

5. What does it mean for God to be your hiding place? Where are some of your favorite places to spend time with him?

6. What do you think it means to pray continually? Is that even possible? And if it's not possible, why would God tell us to do it?

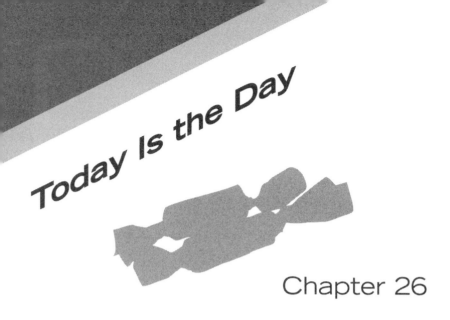

Today Is the Day

Chapter 26

Guided Meditation

There have been many things keeping you from this moment. Your friends don't get it. But deep inside you sense something calling you into a relationship with God. You've done your best to avoid God up until now, but you can't get away from that nagging feeling deep inside your soul that you desperately need a relationship with Jesus.

But what does it actually mean to have Jesus in your heart? And how does he get in there, anyway? Why do people use that kind of language in describing a relationship with God? It's like they're talking in code or something.

Yet there is definitely a deep hole inside of you longing to be filled. You feel as though you're missing something very important in your life, and you desperately want to figure out what it is.

So you decide to get down on your knees (because that's how you've seen people do it on TV) and cry out to God. You say, "God, if you're there I want to know you. I want to believe in you. I do believe in you. I don't know exactly how all of this works, and I certainly don't know everything I need to know about you. But I've heard some people tell me that you died in my place. That was very nice of you. Thanks. I've also heard that you rose from the dead and that you came back to life and that you're still alive today. And if that's true, then I want to know you. I've done plenty of stuff that I'm not at all proud of and I'm sorry. I want you to forgive me. And I need you to help me become a better person."

As you stay there for a while kneeling, you're waiting for something to happen. You have no idea what to expect. And nothing major does happen. No flashes of lightning or loud announcements. But as you stand, you sense something different deep inside. There's some new feeling about all of this. You smile as you think about what the future looks like now that you have a relationship with Jesus...

Journal Entry

_____

_____

_____

_____

_____

_____

_____

_____

_____

_____

Scripture Guides Us

What does it mean to have a relationship with Jesus? How do you start one? What are you supposed to do? Is there more involved than simply praying a prayer and inviting him into your life? What if it meant allowing him to radically change the way you're living your life? What if it meant following his teachings as laid out in the Bible? Would you still be up for it? Would it still be worth it?

Take a few minutes to "chew on" the following Scripture verses, allowing God's Spirit to speak to you.

MATTHEW 16:24-26

Then Jesus said to his disciples, "Whoever wants to be my disciple must deny themselves and take up their cross and follow me. For whoever wants to save their life will lose it, but whoever loses their life for me will find it. What good will it be for you to gain the whole world, yet forfeit your soul? Or what can you give in exchange for your soul?"

JOHN 10:10

"The thief comes only to steal and kill and destroy; I have come that they may have life, and have it to the full."

2 CORINTHIANS 5:17

Therefore, if anyone is in Christ, the new creation has come: The old has gone, the new is here!

2 CORINTHIANS 6:2

"In the time of my favor I heard you, and in the day of salvation I helped you." I tell you, now is the time of God's favor, now is the day of salvation.

JOHN 3:16-17

For God so loved the world that he gave his one and only Son, that whoever believes in him shall not perish but have eternal life. For God did not send his Son into the world to condemn the world, but to save the world through him.

Questions for Reflection

1. Have you ever made a decision to begin following Jesus Christ? If you have, what are you doing to actively pursue this relationship today? If not, what's holding you back?

2. How would you explain what it means to begin a relationship with Jesus to someone who has no idea what you're talking about?

3. What do you think it means to believe in Jesus? What exactly do you have to believe about him in order to have a relationship with him?

4. Some people decide to commit their lives to Jesus because they're afraid if they don't they'll end up going to hell when they die. Do you think this is the right motivation to begin following Jesus? If not, what should our motivation be?

5. Look at Matthew 16:24-26 again. What do you think Jesus meant when he said we must deny ourselves, take up our cross, and follow him? What does it mean to lose your life in following Jesus?

6. In what ways has Jesus made you a new creation since you began following him?

7. According to John 10:10, Jesus offers us a full life when we commit ourselves to following him. What do you think this means?

8. What do you think about this statement: Eternal life begins the second you decide to commit your life to Jesus?

9. Why do you think Jesus wants to save a world that has repeatedly turned its back on him?

True Friends

Chapter 27

Guided Meditation

You've spent so much time together you sometimes finish each other's sentences. You talk about anything and everything because you trust each other completely. You've laughed so hard you thought your sides would split, but you've shared in the painful times, too. You are true friends. What brought you together? What are some of your favorite memories?

Now imagine that person who has become so dear to you saying, "I'm moving away. My dad got a new job in another state, and we're leaving before the end of the month." How would you feel? What would you say? What do you think your friend's reaction would be to this news?

You'd love to think that nothing will change, but you know that's not true. You both say you're going to stay in touch through e-mail and cell phones, but you know how difficult that can be. Your friend is going to be starting a new life and making new friends. How do you feel, as the one left behind?

The day you say goodbye is one of the most difficult days of your life. As you watch your friend's family pull away from your neighborhood, you feel completely abandoned and overwhelmed with sadness. You've never had to face anything like this before. What will you do next?

Journal Entry

_____

_____

_____

_____

_____

_____

_____

_____

_____

_____

Scripture Guides Us

A true friend is hard to find. Some people look their entire lives for true friends. What are the characteristics of a true friend? And what does it take to be one?

Take a few minutes to "chew on" the following Scripture verses, allowing God's Spirit to speak to you.

JOB 2:11

When Job's three friends, Eliphaz the Temanite, Bildad the Shuhite and Zophar the Naamathite, heard about all the troubles that had come upon him, they set out from their homes and met together by agreement to go and sympathize with him and comfort him.

JOB 6:14

Anyone who withholds kindness from a friend forsakes the fear of the Almighty.

PROVERBS 17:17
A friend loves at all times, and a brother is born for a time of adversity.

PROVERBS 18:24
A man who has friends must himself be friendly. But there is a friend who sticks closer than a brother. (NKJV)

PROVERBS 27:6
Wounds from a friend can be trusted, but an enemy multiplies kisses.

JOHN 15:13-14
Greater love has no one than this: to lay down one's life for one's friends. You are my friends if you do what I command.

1 THESSALONIANS 2:8
Because we loved you so much, we were delighted to share with you not only the gospel of God but our lives as well.

Questions for Reflection

1. Has it been easy for you to make friends? Why or why not? What are some of the obstacles to finding good friends?

2. Do you have someone you consider your best friend? If so, what makes that person your best friend? If not, why not?

3. Have you ever had a best friend move away, or have you ever had to move away from a good friend? How did that make you feel?

4. Someone has said, "A good friend is someone who simply knows how to 'be' in the presence of someone else." What do you think about this statement?

5. What are some of the characteristics of a good friend, according to the Scriptures you just read?

6. What do you think Proverbs 18:24 means when it says, "A man who has friends must himself be friendly"?

7. Who are some of the people you are intentionally sharing your life with right now? Who are some of the people trying to share their lives with you?

8. Have you ever heard someone say, "I don't have room in my life for any more friends"? What do you think that means? How does that make you feel?

9. What are you currently doing to become the kind of friend that people would want to hang out with?

10. Is there someone in your life right now that you have a sincere desire to get to know a little better? What could you do about it? Are there any practical steps you could take to get to know this person better?

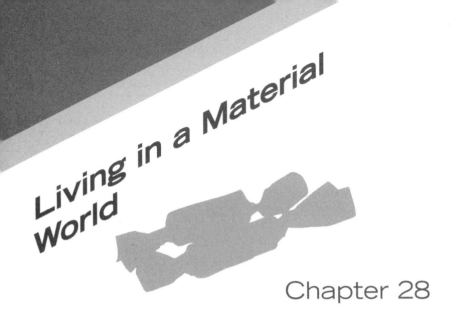

Living in a Material World

Chapter 28

Guided Meditation

You wake up one morning and everything in your world has completely changed. The only clothes you own are the ones on your back. You have one pair of shoes and you've owned them for years. They're tattered and have holes in the bottoms. Your body is stiff and aching because you've been sleeping outside all night under a cardboard box to try to keep warm.

You don't live in a house anymore. There is no homeless shelter. There is nowhere to go to get a hot shower. You want to eat? Then you have to beg for your food. The type of poverty that so many millions of people face every single day of their lives surrounds you.

No more mp3 player. No more computer or Internet access. No more running to the mall to buy more stuff you don't actually need. No fast-food restaurants right around the corner. In fact, there are no restaurants anywhere! What are you feeling as the reality of your situation sinks in? What's the first thing you want to do? Where are you planning to go today? After all, you can't go to school anymore; school's only for the select few kids who can afford it.

You never imagined that people could live this way. That's when it hits you that you've taken so much for granted for such a long time. Do you want to go back to your old life? Do you miss your stuff? Suddenly you seem to have a lot more time on your hands in this new life. What will you do with your day? What are you thinking about right now?

Journal Entry

_____

_____

_____

_____

_____

_____

_____

_____

_____

_____

Scripture Guides Us

The Bible has a lot to say about riches and materialism, and it might surprise you to hear that it's not all good. Even though some well-known Bible teachers have taught that God wants everyone to be rich, that doesn't seem to match up with what God has already said in the Bible. Is it possible to be financially poor and still be exactly where God wants you to be?

Take a few minutes to "chew on" the following Scripture verses, allowing God's Spirit to speak to you.

LUKE 16:19-31

"There was a rich man who was dressed in purple and fine linen and lived in luxury every day. At his gate was laid a beggar named Lazarus, covered with sores and longing to eat what fell from the rich man's table. Even the dogs came and licked his sores. The time came when the beggar died and the angels carried him to Abraham's side. The rich man also died and was buried. In Hades, where he was in torment, he looked up and saw Abraham far away, with Lazarus by his side. So he called to him, 'Father Abraham, have pity on me and send Lazarus to dip the tip of his finger in water and cool my tongue, because I am in agony in this fire.' But Abraham replied, 'Son, remember that in your lifetime you received your good things, while Lazarus received bad things, but now he is comforted here and you are in agony. And besides all this, between us and you a great chasm has been set in place, so that those who want to go from here to you cannot, nor can anyone cross over from there to us.' He answered, 'Then I beg you, father, send Lazarus to my family, for I have five brothers. Let him warn them, so that they will not also come to this place of torment.' Abraham replied, 'They have Moses and the Prophets; let them listen to them.' 'No, father Abraham,' he said, 'but if someone from the dead goes to them, they will repent.' He said to him, 'If they do not listen to Moses and the Prophets, they will not be convinced even if someone rises from the dead.'"

PSALM 49:16-20

Do not be overawed when others grow rich, when the splendor of their houses increases; for they will take nothing with them when they die, their splendor will not descend with them. Though while they live they count themselves blessed—and people praise you when you prosper—they will join those who have gone before them, who will never again see the light of life. Human beings who have wealth but lack understanding are like the beasts that perish.

PROVERBS 30:7-9

"Two things I ask of you, LORD; do not refuse me before I die: Keep falsehood and lies far from me; give me neither poverty nor riches, but give me only my daily bread. Otherwise, I may have too much and disown you and say, 'Who is the LORD?' Or I may become poor and steal, and so dishonor the name of my God."

MARK 10:17-25

As Jesus started on his way, a man ran up to him and fell on his knees before him. "Good teacher," he asked, "what must I do to inherit eternal life?" "Why do you call me good?" Jesus answered. "No one is good—except God alone. You know the commandments: 'You shall not murder, you shall not commit adultery, you shall not steal, you shall not give false testimony, you shall not defraud, honor your father and mother.'" "Teacher," he declared, "all these I have kept since I was a boy." Jesus looked at him and loved him. "One thing you lack," he said. "Go, sell everything you have and give to the poor, and you will have treasure in heaven. Then come, follow me." At this the man's face fell. He went away sad, because he had great wealth. Jesus looked around and said to his disciples, "How hard it is for the rich to enter the kingdom of God!" The disciples were amazed at his words. But Jesus said again, "Children, how hard it is to enter the kingdom of God! It is easier for a camel to go through the eye of a needle than for the rich to enter the kingdom of God."

JAMES 2:5

Listen, my dear brothers and sisters: Has not God chosen those who are poor in the eyes of the world to be rich in faith and to inherit the kingdom he promised those who love him?

Questions for Reflection

1. What are some of the material things you have taken for granted in your life as you know it? What would you miss the most if it were all taken away? What material things get in the way of your pursuit of God?

2. What do you think God wants you to do with your material possessions? Why do you think God gave them to you? How could you use what you own to make a difference in this world?

3. Do you think God wants you to feel guilty about everything you have? What do you think Jesus would own if he were living in our world today? What do you think he would do with his possessions?

4. Do you think God wants everyone to be rich? Is it possible to be poor and blessed by God, or does poverty automatically mean you're living in sin?

5. What stands out to you the most from the passages you just read?

6. What does Psalm 49:16-20 say about our material possessions?

7. How does the prayer in Proverbs 30:7-9 make you feel? How could you begin to make this your own prayer? What impact do you think it could have upon the way you live your life on a daily basis?

8. Based on the story Jesus tells in Mark 10:17-25, how is it possible for anyone in our culture to experience life with God eternally? How does this passage impact you personally? What do you think God wants you to do as a result?

Dreaming Big Dreams

Chapter 29

Guided Meditation

You fall asleep one night dreaming about your life and your future. Try to imagine what things will look like for you in 5 years...10 years...even 15 years. What are some of the changes you think you'll experience? What do you think you'll end up doing with your life? What are some of the struggles you anticipate facing in order to accomplish your goals?

Think about some of the people you allow to speak into your life. What are they saying to you about your future? Think about some of your friends. What do they see you doing in the future? On what do they base their opinions? Do you value some of their opinions over others? Why do you think that is?

As you think about some of the teachers you like the best—those who have had a significant influence on your life—what do you think they would encourage you to pursue with your future? Out of all of the teachers who've had a significant influence on your life, whose opinion do you value the most? Why?

Think about the members of your family, not only your parents and your siblings (if you have them), but your extended family, too. What are your grandparents encouraging you to pursue with your life? What does that mean to you? Do you have other family members (aunts, uncles, etc.) who you could see pushing you in the right direction? Why do you think they have that kind of influence in your life?

Now think about yourself for a minute. What do you want to do with your life? What unique gifts, talents, or abilities do you have that you would like to use in the future? What's your heart telling you to do? And if you don't sense it telling you anything, why do you think that is?

Finally, think about what God wants you to do with your life. What do you think God would say about all of the advice you've been given? God's the one who created you and designed you for a unique purpose in this world. Do you think it would be a good idea to ask God about what he sees in your future and listen to the answers? And don't forget, when it comes to the future, God's the only one who's already there.

Journal Entry

_____

_____

_____

_____

_____

_____

_____

_____

_____

Scripture Guides Us

Nobody knows what the future will bring. No one can predict the future. So we have to walk by faith. There's no sense worrying about the future or being afraid of what it may bring, either. The Bible talks a lot about the future and how we should relate to it as a follower of Christ.

Take a few minutes to "chew on" the following Scripture verses, allowing God's Spirit to speak to you.

JAMES 4:13-15

Now listen, you who say, "Today or tomorrow we will go to this or that city, spend a year there, carry on business and make money." Why, you do not even know what will happen tomorrow. What is your life? You are a mist that appears for a little while and then vanishes. Instead, you ought to say, "If it is the Lord's will, we will live and do this or that."

MATTHEW 6:34

"Therefore do not worry about tomorrow, for tomorrow will worry about itself. Each day has enough trouble of its own."

JEREMIAH 29:11

"For I know the plans I have for you," declares the LORD, "plans to prosper you and not to harm you, plans to give you hope and a future."

Questions for Reflection

1. What's the message our culture has been sending you about the future? What do you think that's based upon?

2. What have those people you trust most been telling you about your future? How does it make you feel?

3. How important do you think it is to listen to the right voices when it comes to your future?

4. What do you think will be some of your most difficult challenges in your future? What do you think you'll enjoy the most about it?

5. Is there anything that scares you about the future? What do you think you should do about that fear? Who could you share your fear with? How do you think that would help?

6. What's your reaction to James 4:14: "You are a mist that appears for a little while and then vanishes"?

7. Why do you think Jesus says what he does about the future in Matthew 6:34? What difference could these words make in your life today? Do you know anyone else who could benefit from these words?

8. How does it make you feel to know that God already exists in the future? Do you believe God has good intentions for you and your future? Why or why not?

Forgiving the Unforgivable

Chapter 30

Guided Meditation

You are on one of the most difficult roads you've ever walked in your life. Someone very close to you has done something to hurt you in a way that you never imagined you'd ever be hurt. The pain is so intense that part of you wants to run away so no one can see you crying, but the other part of you wants revenge.

You can feel yourself getting angrier and angrier as you think about what this person has done to you. If you don't figure this out quickly, you can imagine yourself saying or doing some pretty awful things as a result of your pain.

Then you hear someone whispering to you. It sounds like someone you know, but you can't see who it is, and you can't tell where the voice is coming from. But the whisper is getting through. The words are becoming more and more distinct the longer you listen to them: "Forgive."

"What? You've got to be kidding me," you say to yourself. "Do you have any idea what this person has done to me? You obviously have no idea how much pain this person has caused me." But the whisper is getting louder and louder: "Forgive."

A million reasons come to mind why it wouldn't be right to forgive this person. But the whisper continues: "Forgive." You have no idea how you could ever let something like this go. It wouldn't be right! "If I forgive this time, people will keep walking all over me for my entire life," you say to yourself.

So what are you going to do? Who's whispering those words into your life anyway? And why would the whisperer feel so strongly about you forgiving this person? It seems like you have some important decisions to make...

Journal Entry

Scripture Guides Us

Why is it so hard to forgive some people? And how can you tell when you've truly forgiven them, anyway? Do you think God wants you to automatically forgive anyone and everyone for whatever they might do to hurt you? Or are there certain sins that are unforgivable?

Take a few minutes to "chew on" the following Scripture verses, allowing God's Spirit to speak to you.

MATTHEW 6:12-15

"'Forgive us our debts, as we also have forgiven our debtors. And lead us not into temptation, but deliver us from the evil one.' For if you forgive others when they sin against you, your heavenly Father will also forgive you. But if you do not forgive men their sins, your Father will not forgive your sins."

LUKE 23:33-34

When they came to the place called the Skull, they crucified him there, along with the criminals—one on his right, the other on his left. Jesus said, "Father, forgive them, for they do not know what they are doing." And they divided up his clothes by casting lots.

MATTHEW 18:21-35

Then Peter came to Jesus and asked, "Lord, how many times shall I forgive someone who sins against me? Up to seven times?" Jesus answered, "I tell you, not seven times, but seventy-seven times. Therefore, the kingdom of heaven is like a king who wanted to settle accounts with his servants. As he began the settlement, a man who owed him ten thousand bags of gold was brought to him. Since he was not able to pay, the master ordered that he and his wife and his children and all that he had be sold to repay the debt. The servant fell on his knees before him. 'Be patient with me,' he begged, 'and I will pay you back.' The servant's master took pity on him, canceled the debt and let him go. But when that servant went out, he found one of his fellow servants who owed him a hundred silver coins. He grabbed him and began to choke him. 'Pay back what you owe me!' he demanded. His fellow servant fell to his knees and begged him, 'Be patient with me, and I will pay you back.' But he refused. Instead, he went off and had the man thrown into prison until he could pay the debt. When the other servants saw what had happened, they were greatly distressed and went and told their master everything that had happened. Then the master called the servant in. 'You wicked servant,' he said, 'I canceled all that debt of yours because you begged me to. Shouldn't you have had mercy on your fellow servant just as I had on you?' In anger his master turned him over to the jailers to be tortured, until he should pay back all he owed. This is how my heavenly Father will treat each of you unless you forgive a brother or sister from your heart."

1 JOHN 1:9-10

If we confess our sins, he is faithful and just and will forgive us our sins and purify us from all unrighteousness. If we claim we have not sinned, we make him out to be a liar and his word is not in us.

Questions for Reflection

1. Does forgiveness come easy to you? Why or why not?

2. What's the difference between someone saying to you, "I'm sorry" and someone saying, "I'm sorry. Would you please forgive me?" How important is it that someone asks for forgiveness? Why?

3. Describe a time in your life when you found it difficult to forgive someone. What did you learn about yourself through this situation?

4. Someone once said, "The only person you hurt when you refuse to forgive someone is yourself." What do you think about that statement?

5. How do you think it was possible for Jesus to forgive those who put him to death on the cross? Do you think we're still capable of that same kind of forgiveness? If so, how?

6. What does Jesus have to say about the type of forgiveness we should practice toward each other in Matthew 18? Do you think this is possible? What makes it tough to live out?

7. What does 1 John 1:9-10 say about God's forgiveness?

On a Mission

Chapter 31

Guided Meditation

You never imagined yourself doing something like this. You feel way out of your comfort zone out here on this mission trip.

You have to admit, you never thought you'd be going on a trip like this because, when you heard how much it cost, you never imagined being able to raise the amount of money you needed. But you decided to step out in faith and send the letters asking for support from your friends and family to see what would happen. And astonishingly, the money started pouring in! How did that make you feel? How will this help you the next time you doubt God in some way?

And so here you are thousands of miles from home, spending your days with unfamiliar people, and encountering situations you never could have anticipated. You feel stretched in a million different ways, and it's very uncomfortable. You wonder if what you're doing is going to make much difference in the grand scheme of things. But something inside you tells you to keep pressing, to keep stretching yourself. Even though it feels hard right now, something's telling you that all of this is good for you.

Journal Entry

Scripture Guides Us

As followers of Christ, we've been blessed so that we can be a blessing to a world that desperately needs Jesus. What could God do through you to make a positive difference in this world? Maybe it's time for you to step outside of your comfort zone and allow God to stretch you.

Take a few minutes to "chew on" the following Scripture verses, allowing God's Spirit to speak to you.

MATTHEW 25:31-46

"When the Son of Man comes in his glory, and all the angels with him, he will sit on his glorious throne. All the nations will be gathered before him, and he will separate the people one from another as a shepherd separates the sheep from the goats. He will put the sheep on his right and the goats on his left. Then the King will say to those on his right, 'Come, you who are blessed by my Father; take your inheritance, the kingdom prepared for you since the creation of the world. For I was hungry and you gave me something to eat, I was thirsty and you gave me something to drink, I was a stranger and you invited me in, I needed

clothes and you clothed me, I was sick and you looked after me, I was in prison and you came to visit me.' Then the righteous will answer him, 'Lord, when did we see you hungry and feed you, or thirsty and give you something to drink? When did we see you a stranger and invite you in, or needing clothes and clothe you? When did we see you sick or in prison and go to visit you?' The King will reply, 'Truly I tell you, whatever you did for one of the least of these brothers and sisters of mine, you did for me.' Then he will say to those on his left, 'Depart from me, you who are cursed, into the eternal fire prepared for the devil and his angels. For I was hungry and you gave me nothing to eat, I was thirsty and you gave me nothing to drink, I was a stranger and you did not invite me in, I needed clothes and you did not clothe me, I was sick and in prison and you did not look after me.' They also will answer, 'Lord, when did we see you hungry or thirsty or a stranger or needing clothes or sick or in prison, and did not help you?' He will reply, 'Truly, I tell you, whatever you did not do for one of the least of these, you did not do for me.' Then they will go away to eternal punishment, but the righteous to eternal life."

MATTHEW 28:18-20

Then Jesus came to them and said, "All authority in heaven and on earth has been given to me. Therefore go and make disciples of all nations, baptizing them in the name of the Father and of the Son and of the Holy Spirit, and teaching them to obey everything I have commanded you. And surely I am with you always, to the very end of the age."

ROMANS 10:13-15

"Everyone who calls on the name of the Lord will be saved." How, then, can they call on the one they have not believed in? And how can they believe in the one of whom they have not heard? And how can they hear without someone preaching to them? And how can anyone preach unless they are sent? As it is written, "How beautiful are the feet of those who bring good news!"

Questions for Reflection

1. Why is it important to reach out to people with the message of Jesus Christ? What have you done recently to let people know about Jesus?

2. What type of mission trip could you see yourself getting excited about? What steps can you take right now to begin to make that happen?

3. Someone once said, "You shouldn't worry about being a missionary in a foreign country until you can be one right here at home with your own friends and family." Do you agree or disagree with that statement? How does it make you feel?

4. St. Francis of Assisi once said, "Preach the Gospel at all times; if necessary use words." What do you think about this statement?

5. What's the point of the story Jesus told in Matthew 25:31-46? How do you think you should personally respond to that story?

6. What is a disciple? How should you "make" a disciple of Jesus Christ? What are some of the biggest challenges to making disciples today?

7. What's your response to what the Apostle Paul has to say in Romans 10:13-15?

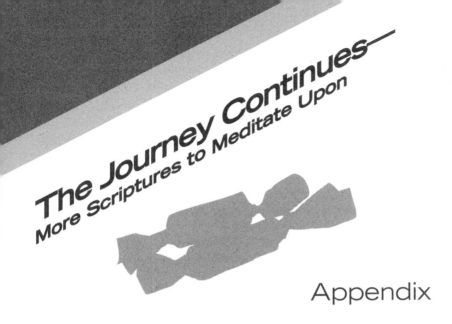

The Journey Continues— More Scriptures to Meditate Upon

Appendix

Luke 5:17-26 (forgiveness)

One day Jesus was teaching, and Pharisees and teachers of the law were sitting there. They had come from every village of Galilee and from Judea and Jerusalem. And the power of the Lord was with Jesus to heal the sick. Some men came carrying a paralyzed man on a mat and tried to take him into the house to lay him before Jesus. When they could not find a way to do this because of the crowd, they went up on the roof and lowered him on his mat through the tiles into the middle of the crowd, right in front of Jesus. When Jesus saw their faith, he said, "Friend, your sins are forgiven." The Pharisees and the teachers of the law began thinking to themselves, "Who is this fellow who speaks blasphemy? Who can forgive sins but God alone?" Jesus knew what they were thinking and asked, "Why are you thinking these things in your hearts? Which is easier: to say, 'Your sins are forgiven,' or to say, 'Get up and walk'? But I want you to know that the Son of Man has authority on earth to forgive sins." So he said to the paralyzed man, "I tell you, get up, take your mat and go home." Immediately he stood up in front of them, took what he had been lying on and went home praising God. Everyone was amazed and gave praise to God. They were filled with awe and said, "We have seen remarkable things today."

John 5:1-15 (healing)

Some time later, Jesus went up to Jerusalem for one of the Jewish festivals. Now there is in Jerusalem near the Sheep Gate a pool, which in Aramaic is called Bethesda and which is surrounded by five covered colonnades. Here a great number of disabled people used to lie—the blind, the lame, the paralyzed. One who was there had been an invalid for thirty-eight years. When Jesus saw him lying there and learned that he had been in this condition for a long time, he asked him, "Do you want to get well?" "Sir," the invalid replied, "I have no one to help me into the pool when the water is stirred. While I am trying to get in, someone else goes down ahead of me." Then Jesus said to him, "Get up! Pick up your mat and walk." At once the man was cured; he picked up his mat and walked. The day on which this took place was a Sabbath, and so the Jewish leaders said to the man who had been healed, "It is the Sabbath; the law forbids you to carry your mat." But he replied, "The man who made me well said to me, 'Pick up your mat and walk.'" So they asked him, "Who is this fellow who told you to pick it up and walk?" The man who was healed had no idea who it was, for Jesus had slipped away into the crowd that was there. Later Jesus found him at the temple and said to him, "See, you are well again. Stop sinning or something worse may happen to you." The man went away and told the Jewish leaders that it was Jesus who had made him well.

Acts 4:32-35 (community)

All the believers were one in heart and mind. No one claimed that any of their possessions was their own, but they shared everything they had. With great power the apostles continued to testify to the resurrection of the Lord Jesus. And God's grace was so powerfully at work in them all that there were no needy persons among them. For from time to time those who owned lands or houses sold them, brought the money from the sales and put it at the apostles' feet, and it was distributed to anyone who had need.

Philippians 4:4-9 (joy)

Rejoice in the Lord always. I will say it again: Rejoice! Let your gentleness be evident to all. The Lord is near. Do not be anxious about anything, but in every situation, by prayer and petition, with thanksgiving,

present your requests to God. And the peace of God, which transcends all understanding, will guard your hearts and your minds in Christ Jesus. Finally, brothers and sisters, whatever is true, whatever is noble, whatever is right, whatever is pure, whatever is lovely, whatever is admirable—if anything is excellent or praiseworthy—think about such things. Whatever you have learned or received or heard from me, or seen in me—put it into practice. And the God of peace will be with you.

James 3:3-6 (speech)

When we put bits into the mouths of horses to make them obey us, we can turn the whole animal. Or take ships as an example. Although they are so large and are driven by strong winds, they are steered by a very small rudder wherever the pilot wants to go. Likewise the tongue is a small part of the body, but it makes great boasts. Consider what a great forest is set on fire by a small spark. The tongue also is a fire, a world of evil among the parts of the body. It corrupts the whole person, sets the whole course of one's life on fire, and is itself set on fire by hell.

IT'S NOT THAT YOU DON'T WANT TO READ THE BIBLE; MAYBE YOU JUST DON'T KNOW THERE'S MORE THAN ONE WAY TO READ IT.

ENJOY THE SILENCE'S 30 GUIDED EXERCISES PLUG YOU INTO THE ANCIENT DISCIPLINE OF *LECTIO DIVINA*. EACH LESSON PROVIDES A SELECTION OF SCRIPTURE, PROMPTS FOR MEDITATION, A CHANCE TO LISTEN TO GOD, AND A WAY TO RESPOND TO WHAT YOU'VE READ.

Enjoy the Silence
A 30 Day Experiment in Listening to God

Maggie Robbins, Duffy Robbins

RETAIL $9.99
ISBN 0-310-25991-6

WHEN YOU THINK OF JESUS' DISCIPLES, YOU NEVER THINK
OF THEM AS A BUNCH OF CLUELESS, FEARFUL, IMMATURE,
DISCOURAGED GUYS—DO YOU? NO, YOU THINK OF THEM AS
BOLD AND COMMITTED. BUT THE TRUTH IS THAT EVEN
JESUS' CLOSEST FRIENDS WENT THROUGH TIMES OF
LONELINESS, DOUBT, AND CONFUSION. SOMETIMES
FOLLOWING GOD IS TOUGH. LEARN HOW TO STICK TO IT
THROUGH THE GOOD AND BAD WITH THIS 30-DAY JOURNAL.

Devotion
A Raw-Truth Journal on Following Jesus

Mike Yaconelli

RETAIL $10.99
ISBN 0-310-25559-7

invert

MANY PEOPLE THINK TEENAGERS AREN'T CAPABLE OF MUCH. BUT ZACH HUNTER IS PROVING THOSE PEOPLE WRONG. HE'S ONLY FIFTEEN, BUT HE'S WORKING TO END SLAVERY IN THE WORLD—AND HE'S MAKING CHANGES THAT AFFECT MILLIONS OF PEOPLE. FIND OUT HOW ZACH IS MAKING A DIFFERENCE AND HOW YOU CAN MAKE CHANGES IN THE THINGS THAT YOU SEE WRONG WITH OUR WORLD.

Be the Change
Your Guide to Freeing Slaves and Changing the World
Zach Hunter

RETAIL $9.99
ISBN 0-310-27756-6

invert

Visit **www.invertbooks.com** or your local bookstore.